Dwarf Hamsters

by

Harry Goldcroft

D1607989

DISCLAIMER

COPYRIGHT

PIB Publishing
13 Pencross View
Hemyock
Cullompton
Devon. EX15 3XH
United Kingdom

Dedication

To all those lovers of cute furry creatures in particular the dwarf hamster. The satisfaction they give you from watching these cuddly little things roaming around their environment.

Table of Contents

Table of Contents

Table of Contents

Chapter One: Introduction

Dwarf hamsters—can there be anything cuter than the little whiskers as a dwarf hamster pokes his head out of his burrow and gazes at you. Despite being a small pet, the dwarf hamster is a personable little fellow that makes an engaging and charming companion.

They are loved across the world and many people have explored the relationship between man and this delightful little rodent. In fact, when it comes to small mammal pets, the dwarf hamster is one of the most popular rodents around.

And maybe it was that popularity that encouraged me to purchase my own dwarf hamster so many years ago. But it was the pleasing little companion that made me fall in love with dwarf hamsters and I have owned them for years since that first hamster.

What I learned through the years is that while these are amazing companions, they come with their own trials and tribulations. As easy it is to fall in love with the little creatures, it is just as easy to make a mistake in raising them.

I learnt through trial and error because I found that there was very little literature out there about them. I combined varieties, which led to problems in housing and feeding. I didn't set up the right enclosures, which led to escape artists, and I made mistakes in the overall health.

But I learnt that despite the mistakes, the joys of owning the dwarf hamster far outweighed the challenges.

And that is the reason why I wrote this book. To celebrate a little companion that really isn't praised enough. And to teach anyone interested in dwarf hamsters all they need to make their life with their hamster enjoyable.

In this book, I will take you through general facts about dwarf hamsters. I will also provide you with a snapshot of the different varieties and will take you through general housing and care needs.

But I also wanted to touch on things that were not as widely known such as providing proper health for your dwarf hamster. In addition, I go over the many diseases that can affect this hardy little animal.

Finally, I will take you through breeding your dwarf hamster so you can begin enjoying generations of dwarf hamsters.

The end goal is to provide you with all the information you need to have a happy companion that you can enjoy watching for hours and hours.

Chapter Two: Understanding Dwarf Hamsters

When it comes to understanding the dwarf hamster, there are actually a wide range of topics that we should cover to understand them completely. In this chapter, I will go over what a dwarf hamster is as well as go over the history and appearance of a dwarf hamster.

Finally, I will take you through general questions that everyone has about dwarf hamsters to get you started on owning your own dwarf hamster or hamsters.

1. What is a Dwarf Hamster

A dwarf hamster is a small rodent that can be found in the wild throughout the world. While they were once a fairly unknown pet, today, the dwarf hamster has seen a growth in popularity and more people around the world are enjoying life with their dwarf hamsters.

One thing that should be pointed out with the dwarf hamster is that they are much smaller than an average hamster. In general, they are about half the size of a regular hamster and there are several sizes.

Dwarf hamsters, like all hamsters, are super cute rodents that are active and playful. They have pouches in their cheeks, which they use to stuff their food into. They come in several varieties, which I will go over later in this book, but all of them are known for their playful personalities that people love to watch for hours on end.

2. History of the Dwarf Hamster

The history of the dwarf hamster is actually quite long and the species has been found through Europe and Asia for centuries.

However, despite having a long history, the dwarf hamster itself wasn't first documented until 1902. During that time, a man named W.C. Campbell discovered the species when he was in Mongolia. It was from that moment, that the little hamsters grew in popularity and today, they are a very popular species.

In the wild, dwarf hamsters can be found in Mongolia, China, Russia and Asia. They can be found in a range of climates including desert and frozen forests and they are extremely versatile.

They are known for being excellent burrowers and will dig up to three feet in the ground. They will also run miles in a night in search of food. What this equates to is an active and entertaining companion when they are raised in captivity.

3. *Appearance of the Dwarf Hamster*

The dwarf hamster is a small rodent that is usually under 5 inches in length. They are known for having a ball like shape to them, however, the Chinese dwarf hamster is longer and less ball like. That being said, the Chinese dwarf hamster is not really a dwarf hamster, just a small one.

Dwarf hamsters have a short tail and look very similar to regular sized hamsters. They have small, curved ears and have cheek pouches where they store food.

They range in colour depending on the variety and have a medium length coat that consists of a double coat, a top coat and an undercoat. They have a short muzzle, small nose and large eyes that range in colour from black to red.

a) Colouring

Dwarf hamsters have a range of colouring from white to black. They are commonly light brown or gray, however, the variety of dwarf hamster, which we go over in the chapter on dwarf hamster varieties will determine the coat colour that your dwarf hamster can have.

4. *Character and Personality of a Dwarf Hamster*

Dwarf hamsters are generally a very friendly hamster that can be quite social. Some dwarf hamster varieties are harder to tame, however, most of them are easy to tame and make very personable companions when they are.

They are active pets and they need a range of activities in their cage to keep them happy and active. In addition, they are nocturnal, or rather crepuscular, which means most active during the periods between dusk and dawn.

Despite this, however, they can be fun to watch and interact with when they are alert and ready to play. They are generally a curious animal and will spend hours exploring new things that you present with them.

Dwarf hamsters love to climb and burrow and they also love to chew. It is very important to have chew toys for them as they have constantly growing teeth that can become overgrown without proper chew toys.

However, in general, dwarf hamsters are versatile pets that can fit into any lifestyle. Some common traits that you see in dwarf hamsters are:

- *Cheerful:* Many dwarf hamsters as described as cheerful little pets that are wonderful to watch.

- *Calm:* Many varieties of dwarf hamsters are very calm; however, the exception to this is the Roborovski dwarf hamsters, which are quick and energetic.

- *Playful:* The playfulness of dwarf hamsters differ between animal to animal but they are generally very playful and will run around their enclosure.

- *Sociable:* Dwarf hamsters are often sold in pairs since they do well as companions. Some varieties can be aggressive to the same sex but many can do well in colonies. That being said, they can also do well living on their own and should only be added to a colony when all the hamsters are young and roughly the same age.

- *Family Oriented:* Believe it or not, but dwarf hamsters can determine family members from other hamsters.

- *Crepuscular:* While some people try to flip their schedule, it is next to impossible to do. Always expect to have a dwarf hamster up during the night.

- *Timid and Shy:* Dwarf hamsters are often timid when they are young or are not handled a lot. If they are handled properly, they can become tame and will enjoy being with their owners. Again, the exception to this is the Roborovski dwarf hamsters, which are harder to tame.

When you are looking at temperament, remember that dwarf hamsters will be different from hamster to hamster. In addition, variety will play a large part in their temperament.

5. General Facts about Dwarf Hamsters

Now that we have had a look at the dwarf hamster in general, I would like to close off this chapter by discussing some of the more frequently asked questions about them.

Do dwarf hamsters make good pets?

Yes, dwarf hamsters are wonderful pets with very low care needs and a lot of reward. With proper handling, they can be wonderful companions that will play and interact with their owners.

Are they good with children?

Some varieties of hamsters do very well with children, however, some are not recommended such as the Roborovski dwarf hamster.

Since they do need to be properly handled, dwarf hamsters are better suited to homes with older children.

Are they clean?

Yes, dwarf hamsters are very clean. They usually spend most of their time awake cleaning up themselves and their home. It is important to note that they will have a slight smell to them, which is common with all caged small mammals. Females in heat will have a stronger smell than males.

Can they live in cold climates?

Yes, dwarf hamsters can live in cold climates and many wild species of dwarf hamsters live in northern climates. That being said, they should not be kept outside. Drafts and fluctuating temperatures can lead to severe health problems for them.

Should I have different cages for multiple dwarf hamsters?

If you are buying two or more siblings, then no, you do not have to have multiple cages. They can live very well in colonies and several species of dwarf hamsters are sold in pairs.

That being said, female hamsters go into heat every 4 days so if you want to prevent babies, never house males and females together. Also, watch your hamsters to make sure no aggression occurs.

If you already have a dwarf hamster that is used to living on his own, you must buy a second cage for a new hamster or fights will break out between them.

Are they noisy?

Dwarf hamsters are not noisy, although they will make the occasional squeaking noise. However, their toys can be noisy and since they run around at night, you may find them very frustrating. My suggestion is to buy a squeakless wheel for the cage.

What is the lifespan of a dwarf hamster?

The average lifespan of the dwarf hamster varies from hamster to hamster but the average is 1 1/2 years to 2 years. Some dwarf hamsters live for as long as 3 years.

Are there different types of dwarf hamsters?

Yes, there are three different varieties of true dwarf hamsters and one variety that is usually classified as a dwarf, although it isn't. For more information on the varieties, read the chapter on them.

How big do dwarf hamsters get?

Dwarf hamsters vary in size but they should all be small. They can range between 45 to 127mm (1.77 to 5 inches) in length. They can weigh between 20 to 45 grams.

How long do they take to mature?

Dwarf hamsters reach maturity at about 21 to 28 days; however, they do not reach sexual maturity until they are between 2 months to 6 months.

Chapter Three: Are you ready to Raise Dwarf Hamsters

By this point, you are probably sold on getting your own dwarf hamster but before you go out and purchase one, it is important to really look at whether you are ready to.

While many people view hamsters as a low commitment pet, there is a lot that needs to be done to ensure that your dwarf hamster lives a long and healthy life. In addition, dwarf hamsters can be around for several years and you should expect to commit two to three years to your pet.

For that reason, it is important to look at the pros and cons of owning a dwarf hamster before you bring one into your home. If you are not ready, you will regret bringing the dwarf hamster home.

Pros of Owning Dwarf Hamsters

Although we can start with the cons, it is better to look at the pros of owning. These are the wonderful traits that so many dwarf hamster owners appreciate in their pet. In fact, the pros of owning a dwarf hamster may quickly encourage you to go out and buy one yourself.

Pro Number One: Easy to Care for

Overall, dwarf hamsters are easy to care for. They generally need the very basics such as a clean enclosure, proper food and a few minutes each day to be handled. They don't require much exercise and do not require long training periods.

It is important to note that what you put in to handling will come back to you. The more you handle, the more your dwarf hamster will be accepting of your touch.

Pro Number Two: Clean

Although all caged animals have a slight smell, dwarf hamsters are cleanly little creatures that spend much of their day cleaning themselves and their habitat. They are not overly smelly and as long as you keep up your cleaning schedule, your hamster will keep everything clean as well.

Pro Number Three: Inexpensive

The first initial costs of owning your dwarf hamster will be the biggest investment that you will put into the life of your dwarf hamster. In general, the big costs are the cage and all the extra toys that you purchase for him.

Overall, you will be looking at an investment of about $600 to $850 USD for the entire life of your dwarf hamster, if he lives to 3 years of age. The first investment is usually around $300 to $350USD but after that, you are looking at about $200 to $260US per year.

It may seem like a huge investment but when compared to other pets, such as a rabbit, which is a lifetime investment of $6,900 to $8,300 or a dog, which is a lifetime investment of $4,500 to $38,905USD, it is clearly a small investment.

Pro Number Four: Personable

One of the main reasons why people avoid owning a small mammal for a pet is because they feel small mammals lack personality. However, the dwarf hamster is a charming little create that will interact with their owners when they are tamed.

They are usually playful and can be wonderful to watch for hours on end. In fact, many owners lose time watching their little companion playing and going about his day.

Pro Number Five: Versatile

One of the nicest things about dwarf hamsters is how versatile they are. In the wild, dwarf hamsters have been found throughout the world. They can thrive in desert climates and have even thrived in climates where temperatures dip below freezing.

While domesticated dwarf hamsters do not have to live outside, this versatility has been translated into where a dwarf hamster can live. They can do wonderfully as a pet in apartments, town homes and large single-family dwellings. They do not need a lot of space and the general rule is that a dwarf hamster needs about 2 feet square of living space to remain healthy and happy.

What that equates to is a wonderful companion pet that will live anywhere you do.

Cons of Owning a Dwarf Hamster

Although there are many pros to owning a dwarf hamster, there are still many cons that should be explored before you make the commitment to bring one into your home.

Knowing the cons of owning a dwarf hamster will help you in determining if you are ready for one.

Con Number One: Longevity

While some people feel that the longevity of a dwarf hamster is a pro to owning them, it is more commonly thought of as a con. On average, most dwarf hamsters live between 1 and a half and 2 years of age. Some have been known to live up to 3 years of age but that is not as common.

In addition, short lifespan of 1 year of age is also not unusual. You have to be prepared to lose a pet that you have come to love much sooner than you would like to.

Con Number Two: Activity Periods

Dwarf hamsters are active creatures but they are nocturnal animals, which mean that they are more likely to be active during the night.

In actuality, dwarf hamsters are crepuscular, which means most active during the periods between dusk and dawn. This does mean that you will have a few hours in the evening to spend with your pet; however, you should also be prepared for noise during the night as your dwarf hamster exercises.

One thing I should mention is that you should avoid waking your dwarf hamster during the day. They often become very grumpy if woken up and can become aggressive.

Con Number Three: Smell

Despite being a clean animal, dwarf hamsters can smell since they will use a section of their enclosure to go to the bathroom. In addition, the bedding that is placed down for your hamster will often have a pungent scent to it. If you are bothered by the slightest smells, this may not be the right pet for you.

Con Number Four: Can Trigger Asthma

One con that many people need to realize is that dwarf hamsters, and more likely their bedding, can trigger asthma in many people who suffer from allergies. Contrary to popular belief, dwarf hamsters are not a hypoallergenic pet and while they do not trigger allergic reactions as frequently as other species of pets, they can trigger asthma.

Con Number Five: Small Size

Another trait that can be both a con and a pro is the small size of the dwarf hamster. While it can be delightful having a small pet, the dwarf hamster can be easily hurt if it is not properly handled.

In addition, the small dwarf hamster can be easily lost if you allow him to have some time outside his enclosure and many varieties have been known to escape the enclosure itself.

Another disadvantage of his small size is the fact that you cannot interact in the same way with the dwarf hamster as you would a cat or dog. You can offer him toys but, generally, they do not actively play with you. But they can be delightful to watch and you can offer food as a way to get them to do various tricks.

And those are the pros and cons. It is important to consider them before you purchase a dwarf hamster. If you find the cons are not as problematic as you imagined, then you are definitely ready to own a dwarf hamster of your own.

Chapter Four: The Many Varieties of Dwarf Hamsters

Although many people group hamsters into a big category, there are actually different types of hamsters. Dwarf hamsters are just one variety and in the dwarf hamster category, there are several different varieties of dwarf hamster.

It is very important that you understand the different types of dwarf hamsters since they all have different needs. This is linked to the geographical area that the dwarf hamster is found in. Some dwarf hamsters are found in desert climates while others can be found in verdant forests.

The different climate will change the characteristics of the hamster as well as the lifespan, feeding habits and habitats. In this chapter, I will go over the basic differences between each of the varieties and give you a snapshot of the dwarf hamster variety.

1. The Djugarian Dwarf Hamster

Also known as the Winter White Dwarf Hamster, the Djugarian dwarf hamster is a small, ball shaped hamster from Russia. They are a very rare breed that can be difficult to find and I recommend buying them from reputable breeders as many stores will sell other Russian hamsters as Djugarian dwarf hamsters.

Temperament:

Like many dwarf hamsters, the Djugarian dwarf hamster is generally a calm and friendly little companion. They do enjoy being handled when they are properly tamed, however, as young, they can be quite aggressive.

Females tend to be more aggressive than males and do better living on their own. They are active and will spend a lot of their time exercising.

Size:

Like all dwarf hamsters, the Djugarian dwarf hamster is quite small but has a plump appearance to him. There is a marked size difference between males and females with males being slightly heavier. Both males and females range in length from 70 to 90mm (2.75 to 3.5 inches). Males usually weigh between 19 to 45 grams and females weigh between 19 to 35 grams.

Colours:

The Djugarian dwarf hamster is found in a variety of colours. What is also interesting is that the variety has two distinct coats—their normal colour and then an all white coat in winter. Generally, however, Djugarian dwarf hamsters do not change colour when they are in captivity due to artificial lighting and heating found in homes.

The coat of the Djugarian dwarf hamster is usually less woolly than other dwarf hamsters but it will thicken during the winter.

There are a variety of colours for the breed, including:

- *Normal:* This refers to a range of colours from light grey to dark brown on the back with a white belly. The ears usually have black edges on them and the face is grey to brown.

- *Varied:* The additional colours include pearl, marbled, sapphire and sapphire pearl.

Lifespan and Maturity:

The lifespan of the Djugarian dwarf hamster is between 2 to 2 1/2 years. Maturity is usually reached between 18 to 21 days of age; however, sexual maturity is not reached until 4 to 6 months.

Litter Size:

The average litter size for a Djugarian dwarf hamster is between 6 to 10 pups.

Feeding and Housing:

Feeding the Djugarian dwarf hamster is straightforward. They eat commercial hamster food and thrive when they can have leafy vegetables and fruit. They do not have any dietary needs that differ from the general feeding, which I have gone over later in this book.

Housing is also standard and they can do well in any type of enclosure. I do recommend against wire cages as their small size makes it easy for them to slip away.

2. The Chinese Dwarf Hamster

Although the Chinese dwarf hamster is not actually a dwarf hamster, it is often categorized as one because of its small size. The Chinese dwarf hamster is a docile little hamster that is not overly aggressive or too active. They can be timid but if handled enough, they enjoy interacting with their human owners. They can be quite hardy, making them an excellent choice for first time hamster owners.

Temperament:

Chinese dwarf hamsters are a friendly little hamster that is known for their calm temperament. When they are young, they can be very timid and shy, however, with proper handling, they become polite companions.

The variety is known to be very curious and they will spend hours exploring their cage. They are often sold in pairs with a littermate; however, females can be aggressive towards other females so it is not recommended to house more than one female together. Males do well living in small groups or as pairs but need to be with other hamsters that are the same age.

Size:

The Chinese dwarf hamster is quite small and the average size of an adult Chinese dwarf hamster is between 82 to 127mm (3.22 to 5 inches) in length. They can weigh between 30 to 45 grams.

Chinese dwarf hamsters are usually quite long, giving them a thinner look than other species.

Colours:

The Chinese dwarf hamster is found in three different colours. These are:

- *Normal:* This refers to the natural colour found in the wild and is a light brown with darker strip on the dorsal of the hamster.

- ***Dominant Spot:*** The dominant spot coat is a hamster that is white with dark pigment on the body and a dark strip down the dorsal.

- ***BEW:*** Also known as black-eyed white, this is a rare colour mutation and results in an all white hamster with dark, black eyes.

Lifespan and Maturity:

The lifespan of the Chinese dwarf hamster is between 2 to 3 years. Maturity is usually reached between 18 to 25 days and sexual maturity is reached around 8 weeks of age.

Litter Size:

The average litter size for a Chinese dwarf hamster is between 4 to 6 pups.

Feeding and Housing:

Feeding the Chinese dwarf hamster is straightforward. They eat commercial hamster food and thrive when they can have leafy vegetables and fruit. They do not have any dietary needs that differ from the general feeding, which I will go over later in this book.

Housing should be in an aquarium or plastic enclosure. Because of their small size, they can easily escape a wired cage. The best bedding for the Chinese dwarf hamster is a timothy or aspen hay.

3. The Roborovski Dwarf Hamster

Also known as robos or robs, the Roborovski dwarf hamsters are a quick, little hamster that is known for being one of the more challenging hamsters. They are known for being one of the fastest dwarf hamsters on the market today and are also the smallest.

They can be a difficult breed to tame so I recommend this variety for those who have hamster experience. I do not recommend them for children since they will try to escape whenever they are handled.

Temperament:

As quick and active as a hamster can be, the Roborovski dwarf hamster is a playful companion that spends its day exercising, running, jumping and playing. They are usually doing something in their cage from climbing and up.

The Roborovski dwarf hamster is usually very timid and they can be difficult to tame. Owners will usually have to keep them under a red light so the animals won't hide when they are close. The reason for this is because they do not see red light so they are not aware they are being observed.

Social hamsters, the Roborovski dwarf hamster does well when housed in pairs.

Size:

The smallest dwarf hamster that you can purchase, Roborovski dwarf hamsters are a round little hamster that is very small. The average size of an adult dwarf hamster is between 45mm to 50mm (1.77 to 1.96 inches) in length. The top weight of a Roborovski dwarf hamster is 20 to 25 grams.

Colours:

The Roborovski dwarf hamster has a large variety of colours and their coat is short and not as woolly as other varieties.

There are a variety of colours for the breed, including:

- *Agouti:* A greyish-brown hamster with a white belly and white eyebrows. This is the natural colour of the Roborovski dwarf hamster.

- *Mottled:* Also known as pied, mottled is a hamster with a greyish-brown back and white belly. The hamster will also have white patches on their heads and bodies that are irregularly shaped.

- *White Face:* A greyish-brown hamster with a white belly and a white face.

- *Platinum:* This colour is a pure white hamster. It is important to note that when young, the colouration is very similar to white face, however, as he matures, the colour goes to pure white.

- *Dark-Eared White:* A hamster with a greyish undercoat and grey ears. The rest of the hamster is white.

- *Husky:* An orangey colour on the back with a white belly and white face.

- *Red-Eyed:* This Roborovski dwarf hamster has a caramel colouration and has an undercoat that is a chocolate shape. The ears are usually pale in colouration and the eyes are red.

- *Pure White:* Unlike the platinum, this is a coat result of two pieds being bred to produce a white hamster with no under shading.

- *Head Spot:* A pure white hamster with a dark patch of colour on the head.

Lifespan and Maturity:

The lifespan of the Roborovski dwarf hamster is between 2 to 3 years. Maturity is usually reached between 18 to 21 days of age; however, sexual maturity is not reached until 3 months old.

Litter Size:

The average litter size for a Roborovski dwarf hamster is between 4 to 6 pups.

Feeding and Housing:

The Roborovski dwarf hamster can be a difficult hamster to feed. They do not do well with commercial pellets and will often refuse to eat them. Instead, you need to provide them with a varied diet of nuts, seeds, fruits and vegetables.

Housing is another issue with the Roborovski dwarf hamsters. They come from desert climates so they need an enclosure that offers the ability to tunnel. They should never be placed in a wire cage as their small size enables them to crawl between the wires.

4. Campbell's Dwarf Hamster

The Campbell's dwarf hamster is a common hamster and it is the most common hamster you will find in pet stores. They are known for having a variety of colours and can vary slightly in size.

A very good variety for children, the Campbell's dwarf hamster can be tamed easily and is a friendly little rodent.

Temperament:

Friendly and sociable, the Campbell's dwarf hamster can be tamed quite easily. They are known for being active but are not overly quick or timid, especially when handled.

They do enjoy exploring and can be curious so it is important to give them plenty of exercise and entertainment. Overall, they can do well in colonies and groups or living on their own.

Size:

Because the Campbell's dwarf hamster can be found in a range of habitats, size can vary depending on the geographical area of the hamster. In general, they tend to have a ball like shape to them that is very similar to the Djugarian dwarf hamster. Actually, these two varieties are often confused for the other and there have been successful crosses between the two.

That being said, the average size that you should expect is between 70 to 90mm (2.75 to 3.5 inches). The Campbell's dwarf hamster usually weighs between 19 to 45 grams.

Colours:

The Campbell's dwarf hamster has a large variety of colours and has several coat types. Coat types include a soft, satiny coat, a sparse coat and a thick, wavy coat.

There are a variety of colours for the breed, including:

- *Normal:* A brown coloured hamster with black tipping on the hairs and a black stripe down the dorsal. Ears are black and grey and the belly is off white with orange arches coming from the belly. The undercoat is grey.

- *BEA*: Also known as Black-eyed Argente, this colour is a cream coloured hamster with brown tipping on the hairs. The undercoat is dark brown and the dorsal stripe is black. The belly is ivory white. They eyes are black.

- *Dove:* A gray-brown coat and gray ears that are very dark. They should have red eyes as well.

- *BEL*: Also known as the Black-eyed Lilac, this is a lilac gray coat with black eyes.

- *Beige:* A ginger brown hamster with a brown dorsal stripe.

- *Blue Beige:* A ginger brown hamster with a blue tint to the coat and a blue-grey undercoat.

- *Opal:* A grey coloured hamster with blue tipping. The dorsal stripe is slightly darker grey than the rest of the mouse and the undercoat is a softer grey. The underbelly is off-white.

- *Lilac Fawn:* A hamster with a light ginger coat with an undercoat that is blue-grey. The belly is the same colour as the coat on his back.

- *BEW:* An all white hamster with black eyes.

- *REW:* An all white hamster with red eyes.

- *Argente:* This is an orange hamster with a grey undercoat and brown dorsal stripe. The underbelly is ivory. Eyes are red.

- *Blue Fawn:* Light ginger with a blue tint to the hair. The undercoat is blue-grey and the belly is the same colour.

- *REL:* Also known as the Red-eyed Lilac, this is a lilac gray coat with red eyes.

- *Black:* A completely black hamster. It may have some white markings on it.

- *Silvering*: This is actually a black hamster that begins to turn a silvery gray as he matures. It can create an all silver coat or a mottled black and silver coat.

- *Albino*: A hamster that is pure white with red eyes. This is actually caused by a lack of pigment in the hair and eyes.

- *Chocolate:* Dark, chocolate brown with grey ears.

- *Blue:* A hamster with a steel grey colouration over his entire body.

- *Dark Beige:* A dark ginger-brown hamster with pink ears and red eyes.

- *Champagne:* A coat that is a light beige. The hamster should have red eyes and pink ears.

- *Umbrous:* This is actually a coat that can occur with any coat type and is simply a grey wash of colour over the entire coat. This changes the colouration slightly such as white becomes a light greyish-white.

In addition to these colours, the Campbell's dwarf hamster can have a variety of patterns and coloured markings on them.

Lifespan and Maturity:

The lifespan of the Campbell's dwarf hamster is between 1 to 2 1/2 years. Maturity is usually reached between 18 to 21 days of age; however, sexual maturity is not reached until 3 months.

Litter Size:

The average litter size for a Campbell's dwarf hamster is between 6 to 10 pups.

Feeding and Housing:

Feeding the Campbell's dwarf hamster is fairly straightforward. They eat commercial hamster food and thrive when they can have leafy vegetables and fruit. They do not have any dietary needs that differ from the general feeding, which I have gone over later in this book.

Housing is also standard and they can do well in any type of enclosure. I do recommend against wire cages as their small size makes it easy for them to slip away.

And those are the many different varieties of dwarf hamsters. As you can see, there are a number to choose from and each one has their own temperament, which makes selection very important. In the next chapter, I will go over choosing the right dwarf hamster for you and your family.

Chapter Five: Choosing the Right Dwarf Hamster

It is an exciting time for you right now because you get to choose your dwarf hamster. Choosing the right hamster can be challenging if you're not sure what to look for.

For that reason, this chapter will go over everything you need to know about finding right breeder, what to look for when you're buying a dwarf hamster, how to choose the right door hamster and whether you should choose in male or female.

1. Finding a Breeder

When it comes to finding a breeder, you often don't have to look too far. Many dwarf hamsters are sold in pet stores and they are often healthy stock.

That being said, if you are interested in finding a breeder, I recommend that you go to a few small animal and pet shows. Often, there are breeders who attend these shows and will have the rare varieties.

It is important to note that many sellers will breed crossbred Campbell's dwarf hamsters and sell them as Winter White dwarf hamsters. Only purchase a dwarf hamster if you are sure that it is not a cross breed.

When you are looking at a breeder, make sure that any dwarf hamsters that you see are healthy. If you see any signs of disease in the cage, do not purchase from that breeder. This can also be applied to purchasing from a pet store.

In addition, find a breeder who is knowledgeable about the dwarf hamster that they breed. They should be able to give you their age, the overall health of the parents and the young and information on proper care.

If your breeder is unable to help you as a new owner, then you should look for a new breeder.

Overall, however, the majority of people purchasing a dwarf hamster will purchase them from a pet store and it can be a very easy process.

2. Choosing your Dwarf Hamster

When it comes to choosing your dwarf hamster, it really comes down to what you are looking for in regards to personality and looks. In general, young dwarf hamsters are very similar in temperament, but you will find that one or two will stand out when you are choosing one.

This could be to how the dwarf hamster is reacting to you watching them or it can simply be a colour or pattern that drew your eye.

When you're in choosing a dwarf hamster it is important to look it is important to look at the establishment that you're purchasing your hamster from. Make sure not the establishment is clean, the there is no overcrowding in the cages and that all the animals are healthy.

When you are purchasing and dwarf hamster, follow these key points.

Number one: Look for any signs of disease

Although your focus will be on one hamster, take the time to look and all the dwarf hamsters in the cage. To see if any are listless, show loss of fur, dull eyes, and if they have diarrhoea or wet tail. Wet tail is a serious condition and if one dwarf hamster in the cage has it, chances are all of them are affect.

If any hamsters appear to be sick, choose a dwarf hamster from a different cage or a different store.

Number Two: Do a Quick Health Check

Once you have narrowed down your dwarf hamster to one or two, do a quick health check on him. Look at his eyes and nose and make sure there is no discharge coming from either.

In addition, check for bald patches of fur and for any scabs. Scabs could be caused by fighting but there is a chance it could be infected, which will lead to health problems in your dwarf hamster.

Number Three: Choose a Young Dwarf Hamster

Finally, choose a young dwarf hamster that is roughly 21 to 28 days of age. When they are older, it can be harder to tame them and establish a bond. In addition, choosing an older dwarf hamster will result in you have less time with your pet.

It may not seem like a lot but when you take these three things into consideration, you will have a much happier life with your pet.

a) Male or Female?

When it comes to choosing between a male and a female, there really is no set rule of which one is better. In general, both have the same temperament. Females can often be a bit more aggressive and usually do better living alone.

Males can be more placid but this is not always the case so don't rely on this trait if you choose male. They do, however, do well in groups or colonies so if you would like to own more than one dwarf hamster, I would recommend that you choose a male.

i. Sexing a Dwarf Hamster

It happens to many first time dwarf hamster owners. They pick two beautiful little companions, the person at the pet store assures the new owners that both hamsters are the same sex. They get them home, life seems wonderful until they notice that Bob is starting to gain a bit of weight.

And then they quickly realize why when Bob pops out a few pups and they realize she is really a Roberta. Although this doesn't always happen, the best way to avoid having pups if you don't want them is to sex the dwarf hamster yourself.

While it may seem difficult, sexing a dwarf hamster is fairly simple and should only take a few seconds. To sex your dwarf hamster, follow these steps:

1. Place the dwarf hamster on his back carefully. You should cup him in the palm of your hand and then turn him over gently so you can see his bottom.

2. Focus on his bottom area.

3. If you see a slightly elongated vent that is sticking out, that has two holes, one on either end of the vent, that you are looking at a male.

4. If you see two holes that are close together and you see four pairs of nipples, then it is a female. Nipples are only seen on female dwarf hamsters.

And that is all there is to sexing your dwarf hamster.

b) How many to Choose?

As mentioned earlier, if you are choosing a female dwarf hamster, you should choose to own just one dwarf hamster per cage that you have. If you are choosing a male, the rule of thumb is 2 square feet of cage for every hamster so make sure you have enough room. Overcrowding can lead to aggressive behaviour and sick dwarf hamsters.

Chapter Six: Preparing for your Dwarf Hamster

Although we have discussed choosing your dwarf hamster already, before you head to the store and pick up your dwarf hamster, you should take the time to have everything set up for him.

By setting up the cage prior to your dwarf hamster coming home, you will be sure to minimize the amount of stress that your dwarf hamster will feel.

1. Your Dwarf Hamster's Cage

When it comes to hamster cages, there are a wide variety of them for you to choose from and not all of them are created equal. Personally, I prefer a modular cage or an aquarium since dwarf hamsters can easily escape through wire bars.

Wire Cage

According to the National Hamster Council, wire hamster cages should have a farce face of 0.8cm apart, however, even when those measurements in many dwarf hamster's can escape from their cages, especially the Chinese dwarf hamster.

Traditionally, wire cages have wire sides and top, along with a plastic base. They offer the best ventilation for your dwarf hamster and they're very easy to clean.

One of the cons of using a wire cage is that they are very messy. In addition, wire cages can be very drafty and it can be difficult to meet the heating requirements that a dwarf hamster needs.

In general, I do not recommend wire cages but if you can find one with very thin spaces between the bars, they are an acceptable enclosure.

Modular cage

Modular cages, some have bars similar to a wire cage while others may be solid plastic with venting.

These are very fun cage for dwarf hamsters as you can add tunnels sleeping quarters and other fun accessories to the cage. One important fact to know is that the dwarf hamsters do not have hairless fingers, instead they have a small layer of fur. What this means is that the dwarf hamster cannot cling to the surface of the tunnel so they need tunnels that have a uneven surface and ones that are level as opposed to inclined.

Modular tunnels can be slightly harder to clean, especially if the dwarf hamster defecated in the tunnel. However, they are a lot of fun and they offer a lot of space for your dwarf hamster while offering him ample places to play and explore.

Aquarium Cage

An aquarium cage is just what it sounds like, an aquarium that has been set up for your dwarf hamster. These are usually very good for dwarf hamsters as they offer a lot of room for your hamster without the worry of the hamster escaping.

Aquarium cages can be glass or plastic and they offer a wonderful view of your dwarf hamster as he goes about his day.

They are usually very easy to clean and they have the added bonus of keeping the mess inside the cage. On the negative, you will have to get a ventilation grill made for the top so there is no way your dwarf hamster can escape while still providing ventilation. In addition, they are very heavy so once you have one set up, there won't be an opportunity to move it.

Overall, the type of cage that you are going to be using is a preference thing but I would recommend using a fully enclosed cage so your dwarf hamster won't escape.

2. Setting up the Cage

Once you have decided on the cage you will want to use, it is time to start setting it up for your dwarf hamster. This is a very important part of proper dwarf hamster husbandry and it can help keep the mess to a minimum.

While many people think of having set areas for the dwarf hamster, they will actually be the ones that will determine where everything is. Your dwarf hamster may create a potty area or he may go to the bathroom everywhere in the cage.

In addition, you may set up a nesting area and your dwarf hamster will decide to place it somewhere different. The best key is to let your dwarf hamster make his house the way he wants it.

a) Cleaning

The very first thing that you should do when you are setting up the dwarf hamster cage is to clean everything that is going in the cage with warm water and soap. Make sure that you clean the cage as well and that you allowed everything to dry completely.

b) Substrate

Once the cage is dry, place substrate on the bottom of the cage to about 3 cm thickness. This is usually called bedding but the dwarf hamster will probably not use it for his nest.

There are a number of substrates that you can use including:

- *Wood Shavings:* One of the most common substrates, it is popular because it can absorb liquid and is usually very inexpensive. ON the other hand, it can be very pungent smelling and can get tangled in the hair of the dwarf hamster

- *Cat Litter:* Some people will use cat litter. There are wood based cat litters that do not tangle in the fur of the dwarf hamster and there is paper based that is absorbent. The main problems with both is that they are often hard on the feet of the dwarf hamsters and they can be dusty, which can lead to health problems.

- *Sawdust:* Another common substrate, sawdust is absorbent and will not get tangled in the fur. However, like cat litter, it does have a lot of dust and this can affect your dwarf hamster's health.

- *Wood Pulp:* Wood pulp is a very soft substrate that doesn't tangle and is very absorbent. The biggest obstacle with this bedding is that it can be very expensive and difficult to find.

- *Recycled Paper:* Like wood pulp, recycled paper bedding is very soft and absorbent. It doesn't tangle in the dwarf hamster's fur, but it is expensive and hard to find.

- *Hemp:* Absorbent and soft, this bedding is not always practical because it is not always readily available.

- *Cardboard:* Finally, cardboard does not tangle but it can have a very pungent smell and is difficult to find.

In the end, you need to choose a bedding that works for your budget and also for your dwarf hamster.

c) Sandbox

In a corner of your dwarf hamster cage, add a rabbit food bowl and fill it with chinchilla sand. This is, essentially, your dwarf hamster's bath and he will play in the sand and use it to dust his coat for cleaning. Although not always, some dwarf hamsters will also use the sandbox as a bathroom area, just keep it clean to cut down on the smell.

d) Nesting Material

In addition to the bedding or substrate, you are going to want to have a nesting material for your dwarf hamster to make his home. You can put paper tubes out or a nesting box can be added to the cage. A popular item to use is a hamster house as these will provide a place for your dwarf hamster to hide and sleep.

Don't put the nesting material into it. Instead, allow your dwarf hamster to decide where he will want to have his nest. For nesting materials, you can choose the following:

- *Recycled paper:* This can be used for bedding and for substrate and it is very soft. Again, as mentioned, it can be very expensive.

- *Shredded Toilet Paper:* Inexpensive and easy to find, it is soft and absorbent. In addition, if eaten, it is usually passed without problem. However, if too much is ingested, it could cause a blockage.

- *Shredded Vegetable Parchment:* Very easy to digest, shredded vegetable parchment is soft and very absorbent. It is also easy for the dwarf hamster to tear. It can be very expensive however.

- ***Shredded J Cloth:*** Another inexpensive nesting material, this is a soft and absorbent nesting material that is easy to shred. It can be difficult for the dwarf hamster to make a proper nest with so it is not one that I recommend.

Remember that you want something soft for your dwarf hamster but don't worry about getting the most expensive product. For many dwarf hamsters, the best nesting material is toilet paper.

e) Water and Food Dishes

After you have the nest area and bedding set up, it is time to set up the food and water dishes. For water, use a water bottle with a metal nozzle. Don't use a dish as it can become dirty very quickly and can also lead to the cage becoming wet.

With food dishes, you can purchase some that are made for dwarf hamsters. Choose porcelain or stainless steel to prevent damage to the dish. One thing that I should mention is that you do not have to have a dish. Most dwarf hamsters will take the food from the dish and store it around the cage. Placing it in a clean spot on the substrate is just as good as using a dish.

f) Exercise Wheel

It is very important for your dwarf hamster to have an exercise wheel to help keep him happy and active. The main reason for an exercise wheel is for him to meet his natural instinct to run. In the wild, a dwarf hamster will run several miles every day.

When you are purchasing a running wheel, make sure that you choose one that is solid and does not have gaps. If it has gaps, it is very easy for your dwarf hamster to slip on it or get its paws stuck in a rung, which can result in a broken limb.

The exercise wheel should be about 6.5 inches in diameter and I recommend finding one that runs quietly as your dwarf hamster will be running on it throughout the night.

g) Chews

The final item that you should make sure you have in the dwarf hamster cage is chews. These are wooden blocks that are edible, which the dwarf hamster will chew.

As I mention already, dwarf hamsters have teeth that continually grow. Having wooden chews, biscuits and other hard things for them to nibble on will prevent their teeth from overgrowing.

And that is basically all you need for your dwarf hamster to enjoy his home while staying happy and healthy.

2. Placing your Cage

Placing your cage is an important part of setting up the habitat for your dwarf hamster. If you do not place it in the right location, you are going to end up with a number of problems including health problems for your dwarf hamster.

Some general rules you should follow when you are placing the cage:

Rule Number One: Never Place in Direct Sunlight

Too much sunlight can be bad for a dwarf hamster, especially since they are nocturnal creatures. In addition, direct sunlight can overheat the cage and can lead to dehydration in your dwarf hamster.

Rule Number Two: Keep out of Drafts

When you are placing your cage, make sure that you have a nice steady temperature. Fluctuations in temperature, both too cold and too hot, can have health effects on your dwarf hamster.

The ideal temperature for your dwarf hamster is between 65 to 80°F (18 to 26°C).

Rule Number Three: Keep it in a Quiet Area

You want to choose an area with good traffic but one that is also quiet. This will help the dwarf hamster become accustomed to people. In addition to this, try to keep the dwarf hamster out of bedrooms. They can be quite noisy during the night and they will affect your sleeping habits if you have them in your room.

When you are placing your dwarf hamster cage, you can keep it inside or in a frost-free shed. They can do very well when they are not in the house but you do want to protect them from fluctuating temperatures.

3. Additional Equipment

In addition to the basic equipment that I have already listed in this chapter, here is a list of optional items that you may want to have for your dwarf hamster.

- Hamster Ball (for exercise)
- Hamster Treats (see the chapter on feeding)
- Hamster Puzzles
- Hamster Toys
- Small Carrying Case (for trips to the vet)
- Hamster First Aid Kit (see the chapter on health for details)

Once you have all these items, you are ready to bring your dwarf hamster home.

Chapter Seven: Caring for your Dwarf Hamster

You're dwarf hamster is home and has begun to settle in. It must be a very exciting time for you and while you need to get started on socializing, it can't all be playtime.

While dwarf hamsters are fairly easy to care for, there are still some things that you should do to make sure that they are healthy and happy.

1. Daily Care

Overall, the daily care of your dwarf hamster if fairly simple. Feeding should be done and water should be replenished so it is fresh and clean for him.

If the cage is starting to smell, remove any of the bedding that is soiled. You don't have to clean it once a day, however, to keep the smells to a minimum, it is recommended that you remove all the bedding, wash the inside of the cage, and replace the bedding once a week.

Daily, you should wash the feed dishes and the water bottle.

If you have a sandbox, sift through it daily to remove any faeces. Remember that this is often used as a bath by the hamster so you want it to remain clean.

When you are feeding your dwarf hamster, take the time to do a health check of him. In the chapter on health, I have gone through signs that your dwarf hamster is sick but overall, you want to watch for dull eye, hair loss, and discharge from the nose, eyes or genitals. If you see any of those signs, seek medical help.

In addition to cleaning the cage, you will want to take the time to handle your dwarf hamster. Give him treats and hold him for about 10 to 15 minutes a day at least. You can also play with him by using treats and toys.

And that is really all that is needed to be done on a daily basis. The rest of the time, you can simply enjoy having your pet.

2. Exercise

In the wild, dwarf hamsters will run for miles every day. What this means for your captive hamster is that he will need to be exercised daily. Having a hamster wheel will offer your dwarf hamster all the exercise that he needs.

Even still, I recommend purchasing a hamster ball and allowing him time to explore the home in his ball. This will give him more opportunity to exercise and you will have fewer problems with him running while you are trying to sleep.

Finally, take your dwarf hamster out of the cage when you can trust him not to flee from you. Do tricks with him, allow him to explore a bed or a table, with you right there, so he can get a break from the confines of his cage.

You will find that a few short minutes of freedom will promote a healthier and happier dwarf hamster.

3. Grooming

When it comes to grooming your hamster, you are in the clear—there really is nothing that you need to do. That's right, nadda, nothing, zilch.

Dwarf hamsters are known for being a very clean animal and they spend much of their day cleaning and grooming themselves. They generally don't need a lot of care and all you have to do is watch them be cute.

Okay, that isn't a hundred percent true. You will have to monitor them and make sure that they are grinding down their teeth properly. In addition, you should check their nails to make sure the sandbox is properly trimming them.

If they aren't you will need to trim them. To trim your dwarf hamster's nails, follow these steps:

1. Wrap your dwarf hamster in a small towel. Make sure you can see his paws.

2. Using a simple human nail clipper, hook the nail clipper over the over the tip of the nail.

3. Make a quick cut. Do not cut a lot at first. If you need to work a bit further back, cut them again.

4. Repeat on the next claw until all the nails have been trimmed.

5. If you cut too deeply and the nail bleeds, dip it into the styptic powder to stop the bleeding.

6. Treat your dwarf hamster to make it a positive experience.

Only trim the nails if you absolutely have to.

In addition, only trim overgrown teeth if it is necessary. To do that,

1. Wrap your dwarf hamster in a small towel. Make sure you can see his head. It is best if you have someone holding him while you clip his teeth.

2. Using a feline nail clipper, hook the nail clipper over the over the tip of the tooth. Only clip one tooth at a time.

3. Cut the tooth until you have the desired length. Never cut the tooth shorter than a 1/2 inch long.

4. Cut the second tooth to the same length. Try to keep them exactly the same length so the hamster's bite is even when it chews.

5. Using a nail file, file the tooth to remove any sharp edges or splintered edges.

And that is really all you need to do to take care of your hamster on a daily and weekly basis.

Chapter Eight: Feeding your Dwarf Hamster

Feeding your dwarf hamster is generally very easy and there are many types of food on the market that can be as simple as putting it into a bowl.

However, before you reach for the commercial pellets, make sure that you are aware of what your hamster needs and if he will eat commercial food. Some dwarf hamster varieties do not do well on commercial foods.

1. The Basic Dwarf Hamster Diet

When it comes to the health of your dwarf hamster, diet is an important factor in it. By not providing the proper type of food to your dwarf hamster, you can shorten his life span and make it an unhealthy one.

For that reason, it is important to make sure that your dwarf hamster has a complete diet with the following nutrients in his food.

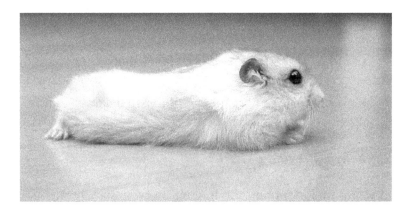

Proteins:

This is one of the most important nutrients for your dwarf hamster to have in his diet and you should make sure the food has a good source of protein in it. Protein helps promote tissue growth and is very important for young dwarf hamsters.

Vitamins and Minerals:

Most dwarf hamster foods have vitamins and minerals in them so you often don't have to worry about them too much. In general, your dwarf hamster will need small amounts but the lack of vitamins and minerals can have some serious repercussions on the health of your dwarf hamster.

For instance, if your dwarf hamster is not getting enough of the following vitamins, you will see the following health problems.

- *Vitamin A:* Lack of growth and diarrhoea

- *Vitamin B:* Lack of growth and diarrhoea

- *Vitamin C:* Scurvy and swollen joints

- *Vitamin D:* Rickets

- *Vitamin E:* Poor skin quality, skin disorders, and poor reproduction

Carbohydrates and Fats:

Another important nutrient in your dwarf hamster's diet is carbohydrates and fat. These are important for growth but the most important benefits of these two nutrients are in providing warmth through fat deposits and energy.

Choosing a food that is complete with these nutrients will ensure that your dwarf hamster stays happy and healthy.

a) Types of Food

When it comes to food, you can choose to create a seed blend yourself; however, I do not recommend it. Commercial foods have been specially formulated for dwarf hamsters and will have a complete blend.

With that in mind, there are two different types of foods you can choose for your dwarf hamster.

Pellet Diets

A pellet diet is a complete diet that is found in a pellet. This is usually a clean food that gives the dwarf hamster everything he needs and it prevents him from picking through his seed mix and choosing only what he wants.

The problem with pellet diets is that most dwarf hamsters will avoid eating them. They do not have much flavour or variety and dwarf hamsters love variety.

If you are feeding your dwarf hamster a pellet diet, be sure to offset the monotony of the food with treats that will keep him interested in eating.

Loose Mix

For the most part, dwarf hamsters prefer the loose mix diet that have a mixture of seeds, grains and dried vegetables. These foods offer variety for your dwarf hamster but it can also promote fussy eating, as some will only eat their favourites.

When you have a fussy dwarf hamster, the loose mix is not recommended since it can create an unhealthy diet. One trick to prevent this is to choose a loose mix that has a complete pellet in it.

Another trick is to avoid feeding your dwarf hamster until his food dish is completely cleaned up. That will keep him from being fussy and will make him eat everything on his plate.

In the end, there is no right or wrong commercial food. You simply have to pick and choose the right one for your dwarf hamster.

2. Feeding your Dwarf Hamster

Now that you have a list of food and you have a number of treats for your dwarf hamster, it is time to answer a few quick questions that every dwarf hamster owner should know the answer to.

a) When to Feed

When it comes to the time to feed, not everyone is exactly sure the best times. Often, it is the fact that their dwarf hamster is already sleeping when they wake up and aren't sure if they should feed him or not.

The answer is very simply, dwarf hamsters should be fed twice a day. The best option is to feed once in the morning and once in the evening.

During the day, your dwarf hamster will wake up occasionally and may eat it. If he doesn't he will eat the morning feeding in the early evening and then the remaining food throughout the night.

b) How much to Feed

Dwarf hamsters do not require a lot of food on a daily basis and it is important to keep their portions small. In captivity, dwarf hamsters can gain weight very quickly and this can lead to problems such as diabetes.

The general rule of thumb is to feed your dwarf hamster two teaspoons of food every day. Break that quantity up into two feedings.

c) How to Feed

Feeding your hamster is very simple and all you need to do is place it in his food dish. He will gather up the food and eat it as he gets hungry.

One important thing to watch for is where your dwarf hamster is caching his food. This is very common for dwarf hamsters but they can forget about their cache and that food can spoil. The last thing you want is for your hamster to eat spoiled food.

As you can see, feeding is pretty easy and there isn't a lot you need to do.

3. Watering your Dwarf Hamster

Watering your dwarf hamster is a very important of his day-to-day care. The reason for this is that dwarf hamsters can become dehydrated very easily. They need constant access to clean fresh water to prevent dehydration.

While some breeders will recommend a small dish of water for your dwarf hamster, I strongly recommend against this. Water dishes spill and this leaves to wet bedding and a wet hamster.

A wet hamster can lead to wet tail, which affects your hamster's health. Instead, use a water bottle with a metal spout. Make sure it isn't' leaking so you can prevent wet tail.

When it comes to how much your dwarf hamster needs to drink in the day, the general rule of thumb is 1ml per every 10 grams of body weight. So with that in mind, your 20-gram dwarf hamster should drink 2ml of water a day.

If you find he is drinking less or more water than usual, monitor him as there may be an underlying medical condition.

4. Treats for your Dwarf Hamster

Treats are a must have if you own a dwarf hamster and I strongly recommend giving your hamster a treat on a daily basis. You can use treats for training or to help with taming your dwarf hamster.

It is important to note that you should stick with healthy treats. Human junk food is not good for dwarf hamsters and diets that are high in sugar can lead to diabetes.

The other rule of thumb is to only allow 10% of your dwarf hamsters daily food intake be treats. Too many treats can lead to obesity in your dwarf hamster. Also, always count the calories from the treats toward the overall amount of food he gets in the day. So, for instance, if you give your hamster a half teaspoon of yogurt, he should only have 1 and a half teaspoons of his commercial foods for the day.

But what constitutes a safe treat for a dwarf hamster, below is a list of foods that are healthy for them.

Grains and Seeds

Grains and seeds are a very healthy option and dwarf hamsters love them as treats. They can be mixed into their regular food or you can offer it to them as a training treat.

One thing I should mention is that when it comes to nuts, many dwarf hamster owners feed their pets peanut butter. While it can be okay in a very small amount, peanut butter can get caught in the cheek pouches of your dwarf hamster so it is important to try to avoid giving it to them.

Safe grains, nuts and seeds you can feed them are:

- Hay
- Barley
- Brown Rice Pasta
- Cashew
- Flaxseed
- Millet
- Oats

- Peanut
- Pumpkin seed
- Quinoa
- Sesame seed
- Sunflower seed
- Walnut
- Lentils

Vegetables

Another healthy option for your dwarf hamster's treats is a wide range of vegetables. Vegetables are a better choice for a dwarf hamster because there is not as much sugar in them as fruit. Some healthy vegetables for a dwarf hamster are:

- Asparagus
- Basil
- Bean sprouts
- Bell pepper
- Broccoli
- Carrots
- Cauliflower
- Celery
- Choy sum
- Cooked potato
- Corn
- Cucumber

- Dandelion greens
- Green bean
- Kale
- Okra
- Peas
- Romaine lettuce
- Spinach
- Sweet Potato
- Squash
- Watercress
- Wheatgrass

Fruit

Fruit is a healthy choice for treats; however, it is a choice that should be given in moderation due to the high level of sugars in them. In addition, some fruit can lead to diarrhoea, which can cause further problems.

If you are worried about diabetes in your dwarf hamster, avoid feeding him fruit as a treat.

- Apple (seedless)
- Banana
- Blackberry
- Blueberry
- Cantaloupe
- Coconut
- Cherry
- Grape (seedless)
- Honeydew
- Lychee
- Papaya
- Peach (without pit)
- Pear
- Plum (without pit)
- Starfruit
- Strawberry

Variety

Finally, you can offer a range of different foods as a treat for your dwarf hamster. Make sure that you only offer these occasionally so your dwarf hamster doesn't get an upset stomach.

- Boiled egg
- Mealworm
- Grasshopper
- Crickets
- Cooked plain salmon
- Cooked plain chicken
- Tofu
- Plain Yogurt
- Whole wheat pasta
- Whole grain cereal
- Popcorn (air popped)
- Whole grain toast

5. Food to Avoid

Although there are a number of treats that you can feed your hamster, it is important to avoid some. The list below is foods that can be harmful to your dwarf hamster and could even poison him. Do not feed him any of the foods in this list.

- apple seeds
- raw beans
- raw potatoes
- almonds
- citrus fruit
- garlic
- onions
- rhubarb leaves or raw rhubarb
- chocolate
- any sugary or salty foods
- any junk food

As you can see, there is a lot you can offer your dwarf hamster when it comes to feeding and you should enjoy meal and treat times with your dwarf hamster.

Chapter Nine: Socializing and Training your Dwarf Hamster

Now that you have your dwarf hamster home, it is time to really start to tame him. All dwarf hamsters are wild when they are born. What this means is that you need to work at gaining your dwarf hamsters trust and making him tame.

Some dwarf hamster breeds are easier to tame than others are so it is important to remember this when you are taming your pet. Look at his breed and if it is a hamster that is not easily tamed, take your time and be patient with him.

In this chapter, I will take you through socializing and training your hamster so you can enjoy interacting with your pet.

1. The First Few Weeks

The first few weeks of owning your hamster can be an exciting time. You have a sweet little dwarf hamster setting up shop in the cage you set up for him and the first thing that you want to do is pick him up and love him.

STOP! Don't touch that dwarf hamster just yet. These first few weeks are very important for making sure that you are taming him correctly. Improper handling and taming can lead to high stress for the dwarf hamster, and this can lead to aggressive behaviour.

Instead of reaching in, start by remembering these rules for the first few days your dwarf hamster is home.

Rule Number One: Leave him Alone

During that first week, do not handle him. This is the time when your dwarf hamster will be severely stressed and he can develop health problems such a wet tail. Instead of handling him, allow him to explore his cage and become comfortable with his surroundings.

Always allow your dwarf hamster to have about a week to adjust, if not two, before you begin handling.

Rule Number Two: Only Handle in the Evening/Night

Although some people try to flip their hamster's sleep time, this is not a good thing for your dwarf hamster and can make him sick. For that reason, never handle your dwarf hamster during the daytime.

Dwarf hamsters are usually less grumpy when they are woken up during the day but they can still be very grumpy...and defensive, which can lead to biting.

Rule Number Three: Place in a Quiet Location

During the first few days and weeks, place the hamster cage in a quiet location where he won't be disturbed by loud noises.

With that being said, however, make sure that your dwarf hamster is in a location where there will be people around him. If you segregate him completely from people, he can become even more timid.

Rule Number Four: Never Remove him from his Nest

During those first few weeks, never disturb him from his actual nest. Instead, wait for your dwarf hamster to come out on his own before you start bothering him. This is for two reasons, one, you will never wake him up and two; he will feel safe in his enclosure.

Rule Number Five: Reduce the Stress

The final rule with those first few weeks, and really any time, is to reduce the amount of stress your dwarf hamster will feel. This means keeping him in a quiet area and keeping him out of reach of other pets.

Also, make sure that he is in a draft free area that has a steady temperature. By doing this, you should be well on your way to taming your hamster.

But while there are rules, it is important to follow some important steps to properly socialize your dwarf hamster.

Chapter Nine: Socializing and Training your Dwarf Hamster

Remember to be patient with your dwarf hamsters as taming is not done overnight. It should be a gradual process that can take several weeks to several months depending on your dwarf hamster.

Step One: Let him Relax

The first step to socializing is to let him relax and become comfortable in his environment. This can take a few weeks but you should avoid handling him. Only go into the cage to place in new food, bedding and water and do not touch him when you reach in.

But don't ignore him completely. Spend each day talking to him quietly as he interacts in his cage. When you place your hand in to offer food, leave it hanging in the cage so he can become accustomed to your scent. As he grows to trust you, he will associate your scent to good things if you do not harass him during this time.

When you see your dwarf hamster going about his day in front of you, you are ready to move to the next step. What this means is that he will play, eat and drink when you are in the room and near his cage.

Step Two: Spend Time with Him

The next step is to increase the amount of time that you are spending with your dwarf hamster. Before this stage, you should have been spending only minimal amount with him—long enough to feed and water him.

After he becomes confident about having you near his cage, it is time to spend more time near it. Sit by the cage and read out loud, fuss with the cage a bit more, but never too much, leave your fingers in the cage for longer periods.

You will know when it is time to move to the next step once he will sit out for long periods when you are in the room.

Step Three: Bribe your Dwarf Hamster

Once he is comfortable with you, it is time to start bribing your dwarf hamster. Start by giving your dwarf hamster a special treat such as fruit, raisins or sunflower seeds. The first step is to place the treat through the bars of the cage. This will draw him close to you and will help earn trust.

When he is comfortable with that, open the door and offer the treat near the door. Try to get him to come to your hand to take it. Do not chase him. If he won't come up, drop the treat and withdraw your hand slightly. Work up until he is taking it directly from your hand.

Step Four: Encourage him to Touch you

The next step still involves bribery but you want to get your dwarf hamster to start touching you. Place the treat in your hand and then place your hand in the cage. Allow him to come up to you and try to encourage him to grab the treat from your hand. This can take a bit of time but you do want him to work up from touching you with a paw or two to sitting in your hand as he eats.

Step Five: Lift him Up

The final step with taming is to begin lifting him up and out of the cage. This is the final stage of having him touch you. Once he becomes comfortable enough to sit in your hand and eat the treat, slowly lift your hand out of the cage.

Do not move quickly as the first few times you attempt this, your dwarf hamster will jump out of your hand. Instead, take it slowly and eventually, you will be able to hold him without him being scared.

It may not seem like a lot needs to be done to tame your dwarf hamster but you have to remember that this is a long process. Don't expect to be holding your hamster before a month is over and some can take two to three months to feel comfortable.

However, if you are patient and work with your dwarf hamster every day, you will soon see your work pay off.

2. Handling your Dwarf Hamster

Now that we have discussed taming your dwarf hamster, it is important to look at how to handle him when you are picking him up.

In general, it is actually very easy to hold a dwarf hamster but it should be something you practice so your pet cannot jump easily from your grasp.

To hold your dwarf hamster, do the following:

1. Allow the dwarf hamster to climb into the palm of your hand.

2. Make your palm a cup shape.

3. With your other hand, cup the dwarf hamster between you two hands. This will keep him secure and will help prevent jumping.

4. Bring your hand over your lap so there is only a small drop to your lap if he does jump.

5. When you are settled, and your dwarf hamster is comfortable with you, open your hand and allow him to crawl from hand-to-hand or onto your lap. Stay alert when he is crawling so you can catch him quickly if he jumps.

And that is really all there is to handling your dwarf hamster. If he is not fully tame and you have to handle him, use gloves to keep him from biting you.

3. Dwarf Hamsters and Children

Dwarf hamsters can be a wonderful pet for older children but I do not recommend them for younger children as they can be easily hurt by a child.

Always include your child in the taming process and encourage him or her to feed and interact with the dwarf

Chapter Nine: Socializing and Training your Dwarf Hamster

hamster. When a child is going to pick up the dwarf hamster, it is better for her to be sitting on the floor. You should place the dwarf hamster into her hands.

Make sure you let the child know not to jump, run, or be loud around the dwarf hamster. If he can stay calm, there is no limit to the bond the dwarf hamster and child can create.

4. Dwarf Hamsters and Pet

I do not recommend mixing your dwarf hamster with other pets. Some can learn to be accepting of other small mammals but they can also get into fights with them.

Never leave your dwarf hamster in an area where a dog or cat can get at him. Many dogs have a strong prey drive and dwarf hamsters can trigger that drive. In addition, cats will often attack cages. To prevent this, keep the cage in a room where it is shut off from any cats or dogs you have in the home.

5. Training your Dwarf Hamster

If you have watched YouTube videos of hamsters, then you are probably aware that there are a number of little tricks you can teach them. This is one of the many enjoyable aspects of owning a dwarf hamster and training them can be easy if you go about it the right way.

Remember that, as with handling, training your dwarf hamster will take time and patience. In addition, you should never start training until your dwarf hamster is tame. Starting before that will make it frustrating for you and stressful for him.

a) Come

Training a dwarf hamster to come when his name is called is more of a condition trick than a formal type of training. To do this, simply follow these steps:

1. Decide on his name.

2. When you have his name, say it whenever you approach the cage to feed.

3. Say his name before you give him a treat.

After a few weeks of saying his name, he should start to come when he hears you. Once he does, start saying, "Goood Rover," before treating him. Eventually, he will come whenever he hears his name being called.

b) Stand

This is actually a very easy trick to teach your dwarf hamster but it needs to start after he begins taking food from your hand.

To teach it, start by placing the dwarf hamster on the table in front of you. Place a treat out in front of him, holding it in your hand, and give the command, "Stand".

When he reaches for it, raise it slightly above his hand. He should follow it and will try to reach it without standing at first but just place it above him until he stands. When he stands, praise him with a "Good" and allow him to have the treat.

Repeat several times a day and he will quickly learn to stand when given the command.

c) Jumping through a Hoop

Another cute trick that you can teach a dwarf hamster is to jump through a hoop. Before you teach this, you need a hoop for your hamster to jump through. Once you have that, start by placing the hoop so it is touching the bottom of the cage, call your dwarf hamster's name to get him to approach.

Hold a treat out at the opposite side of the hoop and encourage your dwarf hamster to go through the hoop. It may take a few tries to get him to go through it and not around it but eventually, he will. When he does, praise him with a "good" and give him the treat.

As he gets better at going through the hoop, start lifting it slightly higher until he is making a little hop to get through it.

Never have it high as dwarf hamsters can be seriously injured dropping from short distances.

d) Wear Clothing

The final trick is always cute to see and it is actually just a condition training again. Before you start, make sure that the clothing you are using fits the dwarf hamster comfortably. Too big or too small will make it a negative experience for your dwarf hamster.

Gently place the piece of clothing onto your dwarf hamster. Softly praise him as you are dressing him and try to keep him happy as you put it on.

As soon as it is on, give him a treat and praise him with a "good". This will help take his attention from the clothing. Leave them on for a minute and then remove them.

When he is more accustomed to the clothing, you can leave them on for longer as you take wonderful clothing of him.

And that is a few tricks that you can teach him. With any other tricks, the key is to use food and to condition him to do the trick. They can learn a large amount of things and it will allow you to play with your dwarf hamster.

Chapter Ten: Dwarf Hamster Health

Dwarf hamsters are usually healthy creatures that do not have a lot of health problems. If they are fed a high quality, varied diet and are kept in a clean cage, you should not have to worry about health problems.

However, despite begin healthy, it is important to understand the health problems that dwarf hamsters can face and how to properly treat them. Catching a disease or illness early can mean the difference between recovery or death.

In this chapter, I will take you through the various health problems that the dwarf hamster can have as well as the signs of illness and first aid for your dwarf hamster.

1. Signs of Illness

Identifying that your hamster is unwell is very easy; however, dwarf hamsters can decline quickly so it is important to monitor them daily.

For that reason, make sure that you do daily health checks to make sure that your dwarf hamster is healthy and happy.

Nose:

The nose of the hamster is often a good indication of health. Dwarf hamsters can easily catch colds and flues and they can contract them from us.

Every day, give a quick look at your dwarf hamster's nose. Is it dry? Does it have a discharge? Is he sneezing?

Sneezing can be a sign of irritants in the bedding but it can also be an indication of a cold. In addition, a wet, runny nose is a good indication that your hamster has a cold.

Eyes:

Eyes should be shiny and bright and should be free of debris. It is very common for debris to get in the eye and cause an irritation, usually corrected by washing around the eye area carefully. Often, when there is debris in the eye, the dwarf hamster's eyes will be watery.

A small bluish circle in the centre of the eye can be an indication that the dwarf hamster has cataracts. This is not something that is usually treated and is very common in old age.

Finally, dwarf hamsters can be prone to glaucoma and this is often seen when the eye begins to swell. You will notice your hamster pawing at his face and eyes because it is quite uncomfortable for the hamster.

Nails:

Check your hamster's nails on a weekly basis. You should trim them but if you see broken or nails that look like they are splitting, you could be looking at a problem.

Urine:

It may seem like a strange thing to check but watch your dwarf hamster's urine. If you find that your hamster is producing large amounts of urine, you may need to contact a vet.

Dwarf hamsters that urinate a lot can actually have diabetes or a bladder infection.

Teeth:

Dwarf hamster teeth are constantly growing and you should have things for them to grind them down. However, even if you are providing the hamster with a chew, take the time every week to check that they are wearing down. If they aren't, you will need to clip the teeth, which is covered in caring for your dwarf hamster.

Skin and Fur:

Another good indicator that your dwarf hamster may be ill is if there are changes with his skin and fur. It is important to note that some fur loss or a thinning of the fur is very normal in older hamsters. It is part of the natural aging process.

When it is abnormal is when it is a young dwarf hamster. Fur loss, and skin abrasions, rashes, bumps, etc, can be the cause of illness, parasites; such as mites, and allergies.

Bottom:

The final area that you should check on your dwarf hamster is his bottom and genitalia. This is often the best indicator that your dwarf hamster is sick and you should check it daily—any time you pick him up.

Some things to pay attention to when you are looking at his bottom are:

- Sticky back end that is dirty.

- If your hamster has diarrhoea. This can be stress induced but several diseases can also cause it.

- A sharp, unpleasant discharge from the anus of the hamster can indicate a serious condition called wet tail.

- A smelly discharge from the vulva can indicate pyometra, which is common in older females.

If your dwarf hamster shows any signs of illness, remove them from the common cage and keep them separate. Monitor their symptoms and contact your veterinarian.

2. Medical Problems

Dwarf hamsters are a healthy little rodent but there are a number of medical problems that can affect them. For that reason, it is important to be aware of the conditions that can affect the dwarf hamster. This will help with assessing a problem early and treating it before it becomes too serious.

a) Abscesses

Abscesses are a condition where an infection gains entry into the hamster's body and a swelling occurs at the site of the infection. It usually occurs on or near a wound.

Symptoms:

- Warm skin on the infection site
- Swelling
- A creamy discharge from the swelling, usually after rupturing

Cause:

Abscesses occur when a bacteria enters a wound and causes an infection. It is very common on wound sites caused by other hamsters.

Treatment:

Seek veterinarian care for the hamster's abscess to be drained. Once it is drained, wash the wound twice daily to remove any chance of further infections. Keep the hamster in a clean cage to ensure there is no chance for secondary infections.

b) Amyloidosis

Amyloidosis is a condition that occurs in older hamsters and can be quite serious. It is a condition that needs to be treated by a veterinarian and should not be taken lightly.

Symptoms:

- Small sized faeces
- Rectum may be prolapsed
- Enlarge abdomen

Cause:

As mentioned, amyloidosis is seen in older hamsters. It occurs when the protein amyloid is produced in dense sheets and this protein is distributed through the hamster's body.

When this occurs, the heart, kidneys, liver and other organs begin to function at a decreased ability. As organ failure begins to occur, fluid is deposited into the hamster's abdomen.

Treatment:

Treatment is through veterinarian care. Diuretics will be recommended as will keeping the hamster comfortable. There is no cure for this condition.

c) Bladder Stones

Bladder stones are a painful condition that can occur in dwarf hamsters but it is something that can be easily treated.

Symptoms:

- Blood in Urine
- Difficulty Urinating
- Increased Thirst
- Difficulty Moving
- Red Urine

Cause:

The cause of bladder stones is usually linked to a poor diet or poor care of the dwarf hamster.

Treatment:

Treatment of bladder stones can be done at home. Often, it is recommended to increase water consumption and to offer your dwarf hamster more fruit and vegetables. A good treatment is to give your dwarf hamster dandelion leaves as this will increase urination and force the bladder stones out of the system.

Another recommendation is to add a small amount of salt and vitamin C to your dwarf hamster's diet.

d) Cancer

Cancer is an illness that can affect many hamsters and it is often first diagnosed by lumps found under the skin. Those lumps continue to get larger as the cancer progresses.

Cancer is seen more frequently in older hamsters and the risk of your hamsters can be decreased by avoiding cross breeding, and breeding siblings or direct family members together.

Symptoms:

- Tumour growth
- Decreased appetite

Cause:

Cancer is caused by a number of factors including environment and genetics.

Treatment:

Treatment is through surgery and veterinarian care, however, it is often not successful. Usually, vets will recommend keeping the hamster comfortable until he passes away.

e) Cataracts

A condition that is usually age related, cataracts occur in older hamsters and worsen as they age. It is a condition of the eye when a thick, grey film coats the transparent lens of the eye.

The condition gets progressively worse and the vision becomes distorted until the hamster goes blind.

Symptoms:

- Cloudy film over the eye
- Difficulty navigating environment

Cause:

Cataracts are an age related disease.

Treatment:

There is no treatment for the condition, except surgery, which is not recommended for hamsters. The hamster rarely notices his poor vision since they are nocturnal animals. The best option is to make the environment safer with fewer jumps and drops that the hamster may miss.

f) Clonic Seizures

Although rare, seizures can occur in hamsters and is actually a hereditary condition. If you have a hamster that has seizures, do not breed the hamster.

Symptoms:

- Uncontrolled urination
- Drooling
- Shaking in the limbs and body
- Opening and closing mouth
- Dull gaze during seizure

Cause:

As mentioned, the cause of seizures is hereditary and can be passed down from parents to young. For that reason, never breed a dwarf hamster that has a history of seizures.

Treatment:

There is no treatment for clonic seizures in dwarf hamsters and it is recommended that you comfort the dwarf hamster while he is having a seizure by talking calmly to him.

After the seizure, allow him to rest. Make his cage a single level cage to avoid injury if he has a seizure when in a top level.

g) Colds

Colds are very common in dwarf hamsters and are very similar to human colds. They can occur for a variety of reasons and can vary in severity.

Symptoms:

- Sneezing
- Wet Nose
- Panting or Difficulty Breathing
- Sitting in a Hunched Position
- Wheezing

Cause:

Hamsters can catch colds for a variety of different reasons, including catching them from us. Make sure that your hamster is not left wet after being bathed and that you keep in a warm area that is draft free. Finally, never handle your hamster when you have a cold.

Treatment:

There is no treatment for a cold, however, keep your hamster comfortable by keeping the cage warm. In addition, give the hamster lukewarm milk two or three times a day while he has his cold.

h) Constipation

Constipation for hamsters is the same as constipation for people—the hamster has difficulty pooping. The poop itself is harder and usually smaller when a hamster has constipation. It can be very uncomfortable for the hamster.

Symptoms:

- Loss of Appetite
- Decreased bowel movements
- Abdominal discomfort

Cause:

The most common cause of constipation is when the hamster eats some of his bedding and has a small blockage. Another cause is not having enough access to water.

Treatment:

Treatment is through making sure your dwarf hamster has a well balanced diet. Make sure he is given fruits and vegetables and add a drop of vegetable oil to his food for two or three days. This will help with the blockage. Finally, always offer your dwarf hamster clean drinking water.

i) Cysts

Cysts are a sac on the skin that is fluid filled. Some cysts can be filled with just air but many have a semi-solid material in it. Cysts can range in size and can enlarge.

Symptoms:

- Swelling at the site

- A fluid filled lump
- Discomfort at the site

Cause:

There can be many reasons for a cyst to develop including trauma, genetic reasons, and infections.

Treatment:

Seek veterinarian care for the hamster's cyst to be drained. Once it is drained, wash the wound twice daily to remove any chance of further infections. Keep the dwarf hamster in a clean cage to ensure there is no chance for secondary infections.

j) Diabetes

A very common condition in dwarf hamsters, it is more commonly seen in Campbell's dwarf hamsters. It is a disease that affects how the dwarf hamster's body utilizes blood sugar. It is very serious and requires management to ensure the dwarf hamster does not suffer from additional complications from the diabetes.

Symptoms:

- Fur loss, especially on the stomach and hands
- Increased thirst
- Sudden weight loss/gain
- Excessive urination
- Fatigue
- Trembling

Cause:

Diabetes is an inherited disease in dwarf hamsters. You should never breed a dwarf hamster that has the condition.

Treatment:

Treatment is through management of the disease. Give them food that has little to no sugar or fructose, this includes fresh fruit. In addition, increase protein and offer a pedialyte solution with the dwarf hamster's water.

k) Diarrhoea

A dwarf hamster can develop diarrhoea for various reasons, one of them wet tail, however, I have gone over that later in this chapter.

Symptoms:

- Increased Thirst
- Loose bowel movements
- Green Faeces

Cause:

Diarrhoea can be caused by a variety of factors; however, it is commonly caused by eating too much moist food or an unbalanced diet. In addition, too many fruits and vegetables can trigger a bout of diarrhoea.

Other causes can be poor living conditions, dirty water or rotten food.

Treatment:

Treatment should start by cleaning the cage and feeding dishes. Disinfect everything and make sure there is no rotten food in the cage. Remove any wet or moist food while you are correcting the problem.

Once you have, give the dwarf hamster weak chamomile tea 2 to 3 times a day for two days. Feed him boiled rice to help settle his bowels.

l) Glaucoma

Glaucoma is a condition that affects the eyes of your hamster and can lead to lifelong vision problems, including blindness. The condition can occur suddenly or you may see it develop over time.

Symptoms:

- Rubbing eyes and face
- Swelling in and around the eye
- Enlargement of the eye
- Watery discharge from the eye

Cause:

There are a variety of reasons why glaucoma will occur in a dwarf hamster. One cause is when a hamster is handled too roughly or when he is held, carried or picked up by the scruff. Another cause can be from trauma when two hamsters get into a fight with each other.

Treatment:

There is no treatment for glaucoma and the best course of action is to keep the dwarf hamster comfortable. Some vets may prescribe an eye ointment to keep the eyes moist. In addition, painkillers may be prescribed if the dwarf hamster is in pain from the condition.

Dwarf hamsters that have developed glaucoma should never be used in a breeding program.

m) Hibernation

Although hibernation is not often considered to be a bad thing, since it is quite natural for a hamster to go into hibernation in the wild, it is not recommended for pet dwarf hamsters. The reason for this is because dwarf hamsters raised as pets do not commonly hibernate so they have not built up the reserves needed for it.

Symptoms:

- Shallow Breathing
- Appears dead
- Won't wake up

Cause:

Hibernation occurs when there is a sudden temperature drop in the hamster's habitat. This could be caused by a cold draft or from your home being under 80°F (26°C).

To prevent hibernation from occurring, keep the temperature of your dwarf hamster habitat at 65 to 80°F (18 to 26°C).

Treatment:

The first step to treating hibernation is to bring your hamster's temperature up. To do this, place a heating pad under the hamster cage. Do not place the hamster directly onto the heating pad and if you feel the need to place them directly onto the pad, make sure you keep the pad in the cage and that you wrap it in a towel to prevent your dwarf hamster from being burned.

As the hamster is warming up, softly rub the hamster to help him wake up. When he starts to wake up, offer him some sugar water. The best solution is one teaspoon of sugar to one cup of water. Give him small amounts of sugar water as he is willing to take it.

Your dwarf hamster will begin to shiver when he wakes up, this is normal so don't worry. After the next few days, give him soft food for the next three days as well as a vegetable charcoal called Carb-v for those days.

n) Mange

Mange is a skin condition and loss of fur that occurs due to a parasitic mite. The condition is very irritating to the dwarf hamster and can lead to self-mutilation in an effort to reduce the itching.

Symptoms:

- Darkening of the skin
- Scabs and wounds on the head and ears
- Loss of fur
- Crusty scabs on the skin

Cause:

Mange is caused by a mite that lives and feeds off of the dwarf hamster. Mites can be brought in by other animals or even in the bedding.

Treatment:

Mange can only be treated by a veterinarian. He will often prescribe Ivermectin, which is administered orally and a cream to help reduce the itchy skin.

It is very important to clean and sterilize the hamster's cage and toys.

o) Paralysis

Paralysis is a condition that can occur for seemingly no reason but it is often a sign that your hamster has been exposed to stress or trauma. The outlook on recovery is not good when a hamster goes through paralysis.

Symptoms:

- Hamster not moving

Cause:

Paralysis is often caused when a dwarf hamster falls from a high location in the cage or suffers severe stress.

Treatment:

Place the dwarf hamster in a warm, non-stressful area. Monitor him and allow him to recover on his own. If he does not after two days, try feeding him baby food. If he still won't eat, then the outlook is negative and you should expect to see him deteriorate farther.

The best course of action in this case is to prevent paralysis. Do not have high levels in your hamster cage to prevent this from happening.

p) Penile Plug

A penile plug is exactly what it sounds like—a blockage in the penis of the dwarf hamster. It is a condition that only affects males and can be quite serious if it is not caught early and treated. In fact, it can be life threatening without treatment.

Symptoms:

- Inability to Urinate
- A white/yellowish plug on the penis
- Squeaking in pain

Cause:

Penile plugs can be caused by a number of factors including the type of bedding you use in the cage. It is often a build up of semen that has hardened and created a blockage in the penis.

Treatment:

Treatment of the penile plug is simply to remove it. Make sure you check the genital area of your dwarf hamster daily. Often, the hamster will remove the penile plug himself but if he is unable to, you will need to remove it.

To do this, gently squeeze the penis near the plug. Squeeze both sides and gently remove the blockage. Once it is removed, add a small amount of olive oil to the area to encourage the dwarf hamster to clean himself.

q) Pyometra

Pyometra is a condition that affects the womb and uterus so it is only seen in female dwarf hamsters. It is less common in young females, however, as the dwarf hamster ages, she will be at an increased risk of developing the infection.

Symptoms:

- Blood in the Cage
- Bloody Discharge from the Vulva
- Swollen Abdomen
- Red Urine

Cause:

Pyometra is an infection of the uterus and is believed to be caused by a female going through heat cycles.

Treatment:

There is no medical treatment for pyometra and the only course of action is to have the dwarf hamster spayed. Her uterus and reproductive organs need to be removed to prevent and treat the condition.

r) Wet Tail

Wet tail is a serious infection that can be caused by a variety of living conditions. It is caused by a bacterial infection and needs to be treated as soon as it is seen.

Symptoms:

- Diarrhoea

- Sticky discharge from the anus
- Slow Movement
- Loss of Appetite
- Lethargic

Cause:

As I mentioned, wet tail can be caused by a number of factors. It is very common when a hamster comes home from the pet store as it can be caused by the stress of moving homes. Actually, stress can lead to wet tail regardless of the situation.

Another cause can be an unbalanced diet and finally, dwarf hamsters can develop wet tail when they are living in poor, dirty conditions.

Treatment:

Treatment of wet tail is through veterinarian care. Never attempt to treat it on your own. Vets will usually prescribe Isonic fluids, metronidazole POM and DriTail to encourage recovery. They also recommend adding honey to the food to increase appetite.

3. Administering Medication

As I have mentioned, dwarf hamsters are usually very healthy and rarely get sick. However, occasionally they will and you will be required to give them medication.

Many medications that your veterinarian will prescribe are placed in food or in your dwarf hamsters water and do not require additional methods for administering, however, there are a few that will.

In these cases, there are a few different ways that you can administer the medication.

Swaddling:

The first is a useful way to administer an oral medication without too much difficult. Swaddling is when you take a clean towel, preferably a tea towel and wrap the dwarf hamster in it.

Make sure that just the head is poking out. Place the hamster onto his back and hold him firmly.

Carefully place the dropper or syringe into his mouth and squeeze the medication slowly into his mouth. Do not squeeze it quickly as he will not be able to drink it fast enough.

Mixing:

Another way to get your dwarf hamster to take his oral medications is to mix it into a treat. The best way is to mix it in yogurt and feed it to him on a small spoon.

Scruffing:

The final way to administer medication is through scruffing. I don't often recommend this but it can be used for both injections and oral medications.

Pick up the dwarf hamster and grab the large amount of loose skin on the back of the neck. Flip him over on his stomach so his body is supported by your palm and his skin is scruffed firmly in your fingers.

The mouth will automatically open and the hamster will lay prone when you do this. Administer the medication as recommended by your veterinarian.

Administering medication can be quite easy and if you have a helper, I strongly recommend it as it can make administering the medication much easier.

4. First Aid for your Dwarf Hamster

The final section that I want to look at when it comes to health and your hamster is first aid. This can be very important for treating minor injuries that can occur. Treating them early will help with preventing serious problems in your dwarf hamster.

a) First Aid Kit

The very first thing that you should do when you have a dwarf hamster is to create a first aid kit. These are supplies that will make it easier for you to help your dwarf hamster if something happens to him.

Items that you should have in your first aid kit are:

- **Tea Tree Cream:** This can be found at most pet shops, tea tree cream can be used to treat any small cuts or wounds on your dwarf hamster's skin. It is an antiseptic that will help prevent any infections.

- **Syringes:** Have three to five syringes of different sizes. You want to have them for giving medication or giving food.

- **Droppers:** The same as syringes, droppers can be used to hydrate a hamster or give him liquid food if he is not able to keep solids down.

- **Tweezers:** Tweezers are often used in a variety of ways such as removing irritants near the eye, removing caught fur or removing something from the fur.

- **Styptic Powder:** Used to stop bleeding if the nail has been cut too short.

- **Nail Clippers:** Another important tool, nails need to be trimmed regularly so it is important to have nail clippers in your first aid kit.

- *Aloe Vera Spray:* Make sure that the spray is safe when eaten but using aloe vera spray can help treat skin conditions. It will also soothe skin when there is a scratch.

- *Vitamin Drops:* Purchase vitamin drops that are designed for hamsters.

- *Heat Pad:* It is good to offer a little extra heat to your dwarf hamster if he is sick so I recommend having a heat pad that you can place under the cage or can place the hamster onto. Never place them directly onto the heating pad or they could be burned.

And those are the important items to have in your first aid kit.

b) Basic First Aid Tips

When it comes to first aid, there is not a lot that I can give you direct instruction on. With cuts, scrapes, bites and wounds, wash the site and apply an antiseptic cream to it.

With more serious illnesses and emergencies, the best course of action is to contact your vet and get your hamster in to him as soon as possible.

That being said, there are a number of tips that you should follow to ensure that you minimize the stress to your hamster and make sure that he has the best chance possible.

Tip Number One: Quarantine your Dwarf Hamster

The first step when you think your hamster is sick or injured is to quarantine him from the other hamsters in his cage. Place him in a different enclosure.

The reason why we do this is to prevent the spread of disease to other, healthy dwarf hamsters. The other reason is that the other hamsters can bully the sick hamster, which can result in more problems.

Tip Number Two: Keep the Dwarf Hamster Warm

Whether it is a disease or an injury, you will want to keep your dwarf hamster warm. Place a heating pad under his cage or wrap him in a towel and place on the heating pad.

Make sure that you keep an eye on your dwarf hamster when he is on the heating pad as they can overheat very quickly.

Tip Number Three: Clean the Cages and Toys

Although this is not a first aid for the hamster that is sick, it is important to take the time, once your sick hamster is quarantined, to clean all the cages and toys that your sick hamster came in to contact with. This will help prevent the spread of disease.

Tip Number Four: Assess the Hamster

Check over the dwarf hamster and look for signs of disease. If it is a cut or injury, you can gently wash the area and treat it with an antiseptic spray.

If it appears to be an illness, do not assess your hamster by yourself. Take him to a veterinarian instead. It is important to have one before an emergency as not all vets treat hamsters and other small mammals.

Tip Number Five: Keep him Comfortable and Hydrated

While you are waiting for the visit to the vet, take the time to keep your hamster comfortable. Feed him if he will take food and also give him plenty of water. If you find your dwarf hamster is getting dehydrated, give him a small amount of Gatorade.

It is important to monitor the health of all your dwarf hamsters if one becomes sick. Diseases can spread quickly and you could end up with a big problem that affects all of your hamsters.

Chapter Eleven: Breeding your Dwarf Hamsters

Having a dwarf hamster can be a wonderful experience. They are playful little creatures that love to enjoy their time whether it is playing with a toy, exploring their cage or stuffing food into their cheeks.

Owning one as a pet is a treat but many dwarf hamster owners realize that breeding them can be as enjoyable as owning one. For that reason, I will take you through breeding your dwarf hamster.

In general, breeding is fairly easy with dwarf hamsters. They do much of the work and you simply sit back to watch. In fact, it is better for the breeder to sit back for one simple reason—dwarf hamsters will eat their young if they feel the young is threatened. Getting in and handling the pups, or baby dwarf hamster, can lead to this.

While my main recommendation is to sit back, I do recommend that you follow the tips in this chapter. There are some things that you will need to do to ensure that both your dam, which is the term used to describe a mother hamster, and pups are healthy.

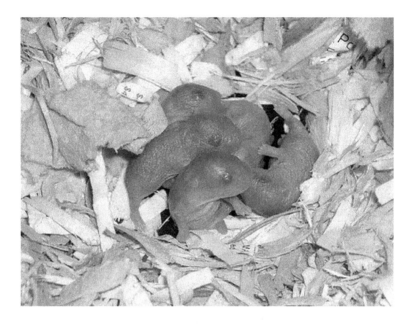

1. Choosing your Breeding Dwarf Hamsters

Before you even begin breeding your Dwarf Hamsters, it is important to decide on your breeding pair. This is an important step and one that you should not just skip over. Although it is as simple as having a male and female dwarf hamster, you need to make sure that you are choosing the right breeding pair.

a) Cross Breeding

In general, there are several breeds of dwarf hamsters and it is possible to cross the breeds. For that reason, it is important for you to decide if you want to keep the breeds purebred or if you want to create a cross breed.

There are pros and cons for breeding both purebreds and crosses. Generally, I recommend that you do not cross your dwarf hamster breeds, although I have seen it done to create new colours, build on size or create a new type of hamster.

However, many cross breeding result in a number of health problems due to the fact that hamsters are found in different geographical areas. These different geographical areas create genetic markers that are unique to the breed and area. When you cross breed, those genetic markers can lead to genetic diseases.

Crossbred pups have an increase in diseases. They are often sterile and they are often obese. In addition, there has been a link to an increase in disease, especially kidney failure, cancer and diabetes. Many pups are born deformed and may lack limbs.

Cross breeding should only be done by breeders with years of experience and should not be attempted by people new to dwarf hamster breeding.

b) Health

When you have decided on breeding, it is important to assess the health of your breeding pair. Make sure that they are optimal health and are free from disease. If you haven't already, read the chapter on dwarf hamster health.

Overall, the hamsters should have excellent energy and should not be lethargic at all. Their nose should not be runny and it shouldn't be sneezing.

In addition, both hamsters should have clear eyes without any cloudiness or discharge. There should be no fur loss and the skin should be healthy.

Starting with healthy hamsters will ensure that your pups are healthy when they are born.

c) Age

Finally, when you are choosing your breeding pair, it is important to look at the age of your dwarf hamsters. Never breed a hamster that is showing signs of age. This can be fur loss, cataracts and overall decreased energy. This is very important for the female as pregnancy can be difficult for an older female.

While every hamster species is slightly different when it comes to age of maturity, most dwarf hamster breeds are sexually mature at about 4 to 6 weeks of age. Some breeds do not reach sexual maturity until they are 8 to 12 weeks of age.

I recommend that you try to breed hamsters that are close to the same age. In addition, never try to breed a younger male with an older female. The female will often reject younger males and she may attack the younger male and seriously injure him.

Older males can be bred to younger females without any problems.

2. Breeding your Dwarf Hamsters

You have your breeding pair and now you are just waiting to breed. Luckily, hamster females come into heat frequently, even as frequently as every 4 days, so you won't have to wait long.

a) Housing your Breeding Pair

Although many people recommend housing males and females together to let nature take its course, this is not something I recommend. Female dwarf hamsters that are not in heat will often fight males. There have been many cases where the female hamster has killed the male hamster.

Instead, place them in separate enclosures. Females and males can live in colonies or groups and do well with the same sex. One male can also live with several females, however, that will leave you with a lot of pups.

If you don't want to breed, keep the enclosures in separate rooms or far apart. When you want to breed your hamsters, bring the enclosures close together. The pheromones from the dwarf hamsters will lead to the female going into heat and getting ready to breed.

b) Heat

As mentioned earlier, dwarf hamsters are usually sexually mature at about 28 days old. However, you do not have to start breeding your hamster on her first heat.

When your female goes into heat, you will notice a few things about her behaviour and appearance:

- She may become smellier than normal. This is due to the pheromones that she is giving off to attract males.

- She crouches low to the ground. Females in heat will often crouch down towards the ground with their legs splayed.

- She may raise her tail. This is a very good indication that she is in heat.

- She may react to your touch. A female that is used to human interaction may react to being touched by flattening herself out.

Once you see her showing signs of heat, it is times to start breeding your dwarf hamsters.

c) Breeding

After your female dwarf hamster goes into heat, it is time to put the pair together. Never place the male dwarf hamster into the female's enclosure. This can actually cause a serious fight to occur as the female is more likely to attack a male that enters her territory.

Instead, place the female into the male's enclosure. Do this in the early evening so you can watch the pair together. As you know, hamsters are active during the evening and at night so it is important to place them together during this time.

When you put the female into the male's enclosure, watch them for a few hours. Usually, the first few minutes to an hour is spent with the male and female sparring. This is more of a tussle and not a major fight. If you see a fight where the female begins to hurt the male, immediately remove the female from the cage.

In addition, if the female does not start to settle down, remove her. This is a clear indication that she is not ready to be bred.

If she is ready to breed, you can wait until they mate. Although it may be tempting to remove the female immediately after mating, do not. It is important to keep the pair together for a little while as they may mate again. Keep them together overnight or for several hours.

Remove the female. You can try to place her with the male again, however, it is usually not necessary and not something I would recommend after a successful mating.

If a mating did not occur, remove the female and try again the next day. It could be simply that she is not fully in heat and not ready to breed. Repeat for two or three days. If there is still nothing, wait a few days until her next heat begins.

d) After Mating

After your male and female have successfully mated, it is time to wait for your pups to be born. Immediately after mating, isolate your female. Do not keep her with the male as some male dwarf hamsters will eat their young.

Care of your pregnant hamster is no different than when she wasn't pregnant. Give her high quality food and offer her a variety. In addition, make sure she has constant access to clean, drinking water.

Finally, make sure she has the bedding and space to create a burrow to deliver her pups.

3. Birthing your Pups

For many new to dwarf hamster breeding, there may not be a lot of signs that your dwarf hamster is pregnant. If she goes into heat after four days post breeding, then chances are she is not pregnant.

The gestation period for dwarf hamsters can vary but expect a litter 18 to 22 days after breeding. During the three weeks leading up to her whelping date, you may see the following behaviours and physical cues:

- She begins to look fatter and has developed saddlebags on the sides of her stomach.

- She is more aggressive than usual. At this point, she may not be able to be around any other hamster regardless of sex.

- She will have an increase in appetite and will spend a lot of her time eating.

- She has a decrease in energy and you will see her exercising less.

- She begins to build a nest in her enclosure. This is usually when you can expect birth to be imminent.

- She will spend more time grooming herself.

- She will be alert, restless and may startle easily.

During this time, you should avoid handling the female too much as this can stress her. Also, start watching for pups, especially around 18 days gestation.

When she goes into labour, you will become restless as she wanders around her enclosure. She will then go into her nesting area and her sides will begin to clench as she heaves. The pups will begin to be born, and you will usually see one pup every 10 to 30 minutes.

In between the arrival of each pup, you will see the female resting or cleaning up the afterbirth and the pups. You do not have to clean up anything or become involved in any way. The female will do it all and if you interact, you could cause her to eat her young.

The only thing that you should do is to make sure that she has food and water as she will be very hungry after her pups are born.

When the pups are born, they are completely helpless and are covered in a skin like membrane called a caul. They are born without fur and are deaf and blind. The female may not deliver all of her young in the nest and you may see them scattered around the cage. Do not move those pups to the nest. The mother will do that eventually.

She will also eat the caul, afterbirth and all of the membranes from the delivery. Do not prevent this as these provide her with very important nutrients that will help her feed her young.

When she begins to bring the pups into the nest, she will pick them up in her mouth. It may look like she is trying to eat her young but don't worry, the female will know what she is doing.

In addition, be prepared for her to eat her young. This is something that happens in many litters and a female may devour weak or unhealthy young. She will also cull her litter so it is small enough for her to care for. Do not stop the female. Interfering could cause her to eat all of the young.

In general, your role as a breeder stopped when you placed the female into her own enclosure for her pregnancy. The female will do all of the work when she is delivering and raising the young.

Dwarf hamsters usually have litters of 6 to 12 pups but it is not uncommon to have a litter of up to 18 pups.

4. Raising Pups

Raising pups is actually a very easy task and there is not much that you need to do. It is important to have a clean cage prior to when the pups are born. The cleaner the cage, the healthier your pups will be. Also, make sure that she has nesting materials such as toilet paper.

During the first two weeks of life, you should not do anything. Don't open the cage but simply provide food and water for the dwarf hamster in trays that can be easily filled without disturbing the cage.

If you see a pup that is away from the nest, do not move it back to the nest in those first 10 to 14 days. The mother will get it.

Disturbing the cage and not providing the mother with ample food and water can result in her killing the pups in an effort to protect them. Hamsters that feel threatened defend her litter in this manner.

Still, even without getting involved, the development of the pups is wonderful to watch and the female won't keep them hidden. By day three, fur begins to appear and you will begin to see a dark covering on them. The ears will also start to become erect on day three.

On day five, you will start to see markings; however, lighter coloured pups will only begin showing fur on day five. Despite still being blind, the tiny hamsters will begin exploring their cage and may even begin trying to drink water so I recommend lowering the water for them to reach it.

By day eighth, the pups will be moving around more and they will begin to nibble on food. They are still blind but they will usually have no difficulty getting around.

The thirteenth day usually marks when the pups' eyes begin to open. This is a good indication for getting into the cage and starting to interact with your baby dwarf hamsters.

Start by doing a thorough cleaning of the cage at this time. The mother will be confident enough with the health of her pups that interactions will not cause her to kill her young.

When it comes to weaning the pups, there is very little you need to do. The mother dwarf hamster will begin weaning the pups at 7 days old when she begins to take solid food to the nest. She will continue to cut them off of milk until they are fully weaned at 18 to 21 days of age.

When she is weaning them, you can add cucumber, carrots and other treats to the food dish. She will give the pups these treats as well as regular food.

By 21 to 28 days of age, you have your hamsters and they will soon be sexually mature. Take the time to sex the pups and then separate them into male and female enclosures.

If you plan on breeding your female again, give her a week or two, after the pups are removed from her, before you breed her again.

5. Fostering a Pup

Orphan pups are not a common occurrence but it can happen. Usually, orphaned hamsters occur due to the mother escaping her cage or dying. Hamsters do not usually reject their pups, although they will go on a walk about away from them. If the dwarf hamster has escaped her cage, try to set a live trap. Also, do not clean the cage. She may come back if she can smell them.

At that time you discover the pups are orphaned, you will be forced with the decision of trying to foster the pups or letting the pups be culled by the mother or natural selection.

It is a difficult decision but fostering a pup can be quite hard and the success generally relies on the age of the pups.

If the pups are under 10 days of age, your best option is to try and get another mother to adopt them. They need mother's milk to survive and without a mother hamster readily available, the pups will die.

To try an adoption, you will need to remove the pups from the cage. Try to clean them so there is no residue from the nest left on them. Place each pup into a cotton towel and rub them gently. This will help warm them up as they are probably cold and will also get them wiggling and moving.

Take some of the nesting material that is in the new cage and place it around the orphans. This will help the pups take on the smells of the new mother. Do this outside of the cage as doing it in the cage will cause the mother unnecessary stress and may cause more harm than good.

When the dwarf hamster pups are ready, take a treat and try to entice the adoptive mother to eat the treat. If you can get her attention focused on the treat, you are ready to add the new pups.

Place the squirming pups, nesting materials and all, into an enclosure with the mother. Place them into the nest and not away from the nest.

It is important to pair pups that are close to the same age. If the mother's pups are older or younger than a day or two, the adoptive mom will reject the pup.

Don't let the mother back at the nest right away; keep feeding her treats until the orphaned pups have wiggled into the group of her pups.

After the orphans are in the nest, close up the cage and avoid looking in for a week. Fostering is completely up to the adoptive mom and there is nothing you can do to change that.

In many cases, the dwarf hamster mom will simply accept the pups and raise them as her own. In other cases, however, the mother will know that the new pups are intruders and will kill them. Don't try to stop her if this happens.

After a week, check in and whether she is raising them on her own or not, continue as you would raising a normal litter.

If you try to foster them on your own, you will need to find KMR, which is a milk replacer for kittens. Until they are 12 days old, it is important to feed them from an eyedropper every hour. Keep track of when you feed them and how much. In general, you will need to give them 3 drops of KMR.

At 7 days of age, you can begin to slowly give them solid food, like a mother dwarf hamster would but still keep up the same feeding times and amounts. At 12 days, the amount can drop to .5 to 1ml every 2 to 3 hours. They should have constant access to solid food and water during this time as well.

At 21 days, you can stop giving them KMR as they will be completely weaned at this point.

After every feeding for those 21 days, take the time to stimulate the pup so he will urinate and defecate. To do this, pick the pup up and gently rub the genital area with a moist cloth. Dry the area as wet bottoms can lead to health problems.

The cage should be kept warm and you can do this by placing a heating pad, set to low under the tank. Make a nest by using shredded toilet paper and clean it when it is dirty.

Caring for an abandoned litter of pups can be difficult and it is very time consuming but it can be very rewarding seeing those pups grow up and go off to their new homes.

Chapter Twelve: Common Terms

While you may not realize it, there are a large number of terms that you can use when you are discussing hamsters, especially the world of dwarf hamsters.

Although you can navigate the world of dwarf hamsters without knowing these terms, I do recommend being familiar with them.

Albino: This is a genetic condition where there is a lack of pigmentation in the hair and the eyes. This creates a white look to the hamster in the fur and pink eyes.

Agouti: A term that refers to the natural or wild colour found in the species. Also known as normal.

Angora: A hair type in the hamster that is long and soft. The long hair usually starts at the nape of the neck and ends at the tail.

Anophthalmic: Refers to an animal that has no eyes and is completely white. Also known as an eyeless white.

Aquarium: A secure cage for a hamster that has glass sides and a secure lid. More commonly used for fish.

Bedding: A substance, such as wood shavings, that is scattered on the bottom of the hamster cage. Used for burrowing in or even toileting.

Brindling: Darker hairs on the animal that creates a striping pattern on the fur.

Burrow: The tunnel or hole that is where the hamster sleeps or takes refuge in.

Cannibalism: The act where one animal eats another from its species. This can be commonly seen when a female hamster will eat its young due to starvation, disease or threats to the hamster and her young.

Cheek Pouches: The small pouch on either side of the hamster's mouth here the hamster is able to carry food, and other items in its mouth. It is interesting to note that hamster cheeks are dry.

Chew Toys: Various toys that are placed in the hamster cage so the hamster can chew them to wear down his teeth.

Colony: Refers to a group of hamsters who live together. Often, the group consists of one male with several females, however, it is not uncommon to see a colony with only one sex or the other.

Crepuscular: Refers to an animal that is the most active between the hours of dusk and dawn.

Culling: A term used to describe the practice of killing sick or weak pups from a litter. Usually done by the dam of the litter.

Daily Diet: Refers to the food that a hamster should eat in a day, including seeds, grains and vegetables.

Dam: Refers to a female hamster who is a mother.

Ectoparasites: Parasites that live outside the animal, usually on the body.

Exercise Wheel: A toy that you place in the hamster cage so the hamster is able to run and exercise.

Endoparasites: Parasites that live inside an animal.

Eyeless White: Refers to an animal that has no eyes and is completely white. Also known as an anophthalmic.

Food Bowl: The bowl where you place the hamster's food.

Genotype: The overall genetic makeup of an animal.

Genus: Group of animals or animal species that are closely related.

Gestation: The time period starting from the time of conception until the hamster gives birth.

Golden: A colour in hamsters that is a gold or yellow colour. One of the original colours of the Syrian hamster.

Hamster: the name of a group of rodents that have a short tail, cheek pouches and are small. They come from the subfamily Cricetinae and are a Eurasian rodent that is commonly kept as a pet.

Hamsterproof: A term used to describe when a room has been made safe for a hamster to run around in.

Heat: The period of time when a female hamster is sexually excited and is receptive to mating. This is the period of time right before a female hamster ovulates.

Heat Stroke: When a hamster is exposed to extreme heat and its body temperature rises. It can be deadly if not treated immediately. Also known as Sleeper Disease.

Hibernation: When an animal enters a comatose or near comatose state during the colder winter months. It is important to note that most animals hibernating do not sleep the entire time they are in hibernation.

Hip Spots: Found on the hamsters' hips, hip spots are glands that are used for marking territory.

Hybrid: The offspring of two hamsters that are from two different species.

Inbreeding: When two animals are bred together when they are closely related, such as cousin-to-cousin.

Incisors: The front teeth of a hamster. It is important to note that incisors grow continuously in hamsters.

Line: Refers to the generations of a hamster. Father, mother, grandparents and so on.

Line breeding: When two animals are bred together when they are closely related

Litter: A group of baby hamsters, also known as pups, that were produced during a single birth.

Longevity: Refers to the lifespan.

Nagging: When a hamster continually chews on the bars of a cage.

Nest Box: An area in the hamster cage where a hamster can feel safe and secure. Usually a cardboard, wood or plastic box.

Nocturnal: An animal that is active during the night but sleeps during the day.

Normal: A term used to describe the wild colour of a hamster.

Oestrus: The period of time that a female hamster will accept a male hamster.

Oestrus Cycle: The breeding cycle of a female hamster, usually lasting 4 days.

Overshot: A term used to describe the bite of a hamster when the upper incisors overlap the bottom jaw.

Parasite: Refers to an organism that lives on a host animal.

Phenotype: The overall physical appearance of the animal.

Plastic Cage: A type of cage that a hamster lives in. Usually have plastic tunnels and tubes for the hamster to play in.

Pregnancy: The time period starting from the time of conception until the hamster gives birth.

Pup: A baby hamster.

Rodent: Any mammal that is found in the order of Rodentia and share the same trait of continuously growing teeth that are self-sharpening.

Run-about Ball: A plastic ball that is fully enclosed, with breathing holes, for the hamster to exercise in when he is not in his cage.

Silbings: Two or more hamsters that have the same parents.

Sire: The male hamster that fathers a litter.

Sleeper Disease: When a hamster is exposed to extreme heat and its body temperature rises. It can be deadly if not treated immediately. Also known as Heat Stroke.

Split: Used to describe any hamster who has parents that were different colours or varieties.

Sport: Refers to any hamster that is different than the norm.

Stand: A female that is in heat and presents herself to a male.

Steppe: A plain that is grass covered and is an ideal habitat for a hamster.

Tame: Refers to a hamster that will not bite when he is held.

Variety: Refers to the coat and colour of a hamster.

Wean: The act of switching a pup from milk to solid foods.

Wire Cage: A type of cage that a hamster lives in with wire sides and roof and a solid floor.

CPSIA information can be obtained
at www.ICGtesting.com
Printed in the USA
LVHW081245220122
709111LV00001B/33